AF568148

HUMAN RIGHTS MANAGEMENT AFTER GLOBALIZATION

HUMAN RIGHTS MANAGEMENT AFTER GLOBALIZATION

Editor

Dr. Rabi Narayana Misra

DISCOVERY PUBLISHING HOUSE PVT. LTD.
INDIA

Published by:

Namit Wasan

DISCOVERY PUBLISHING HOUSE PVT. LTD.
4383/4B, Ansari Road, Darya Ganj
New Delhi-110 002 (India)
Phone : +91-11-23279245; 23253475; 43596065
E-mail : discoverybooksindia@gmail.com
discoverypublishinghouse@gmail.com
namitwasan9@gmail.com
web : www.discoverypublishinggroup.com

***First Edition:* 2019**

ISBN: 978-93-88854-05-4

Human Rights Management After Globalization

Printed at:
Infinity Imaging Systems
Delhi

Preface

Human Rights are generally defined as the rights which every human being is entitled to enjoy and to have protected, human rights means the rights relating to life, liberty, equality and dignity of the individual guaranteed under the constitution. Global development is sometimes viewed as being responsible for damaging human rights. The development of human rights depends on liberal ideas. The economic freedom is one of the reasons for growth of human rights. Development poses challenges to national and international laws. The global culture promotes the uniform cultural values all over the nation. Globalizations causes increasing mobility of job directly and product at lower prices which causes upliftment of state of living of people and it provide job indirectly.

This book will help politicians Government citizens of India, teachers scholars, NGOs and others at large.

Dr. R.N. Misra

Acknowledgement

I am very much thankful to all paper contributors to edit this book. I am also obliged to the principal and members of staff of Government Degree College, Ravulapalem, A.P. for conducting National seminar.

I am also thankful to my wife Smt. Swarna Prava Misra, and my two sons Roopesh and Rookesh for helping me for editing this book.

I also extend my heart-felt thanks to Mr. Tilak Wasan, the key man of Discovery Publishing House Pvt. Ltd. New Delhi, for his kind co-operation and help for publishing this book. I am also thankful to Mr. Namit Wasan and his team of members to take active part in publishing the book in time.

Dr. Rabi Narayana Misra

Contents

Preface

Acknowledgement

1. Empowerment of Women: A Socio-legal Study 1

   Dr. Puspanjali Padhal Retd. Principal and Prof. Dr. Binayak Patnaik Director

2. Globalization and its Impact on Human Rights 16

   Roopesh Kumar Misra and N. Rajasekhar Rao

3. Critical Evaluation of Children Rights in India 25

   Dr. (Prof.) R.P. Sharma and Dr. Mukku Syam Babu

4. Impact of Globalisation on Human Rights: An Overview 32

   Dr. S. Durga and B. Ratnavalli

5. Human Rights for Children's in India 44

   Dr. Rabi N. Misra and Dr. K. Ratna Manikyam

6. Human Rights and the Indian Constitution 53

   Smt. Bandita Panda and P.L. Naidu

7. Human Rights for Women in India 66

   Dr. S. Badtiya and V.V. Satya

8. Development and Human Rights 76

   D.G. Chandrayya and Lt. K. Venkata Rao

9. Human Rights in Contemporary India: Issues and Challenges 82

   Dr. B.R. Prasad Reddy and Dr. R.N. Misra

10. Women Empowerment in India 100

Dr. Brajamohan Sasmal

11. Child Labour in India: A Human Rights Perspective 111

Dr. P. Shanmukha Rao

12. Role of Madduri Annapurnayya in Andhra Socialist Movement 123

Dr. B. Raja Rao

13. Human Rights After Globalization in India 130

Dr. G. Chandrayya and Dr. Rookesh K. Misra

14. Economic Development and Human Rights 142

S. Venugopal

15. The Role of Civil Society in Protecting the Human Rights 146

P. Aravind Swamy

16. Are Human Rights Needed when Human is Being in Human 151

Dr. J. Sanath Kumar

17. Forces Influencing Human Rights in India 154

Dr. G. Swathi and G. Tirumala Vasu Deva Rao

18. Human Rights Vs. Women Rights 159

T. Sreevaram and Dr. R.N. Misra

19. Constitutional and Legal Rights to Women in India 163

R.J.L.P. Priyanka, III BA

20. Women and Human Rights in India 168

M. Swarnalatha, M.A., M.Phil.

21. Human Rights in India 173

Dr. P. Sunanda Vijaya Lakshmi and Amnuta Rani Misra

Index 183

Human Rights Management after Globalization **Pages 1-15**
Edited by: Dr. Rabi Narayana Misra
ISBN: 978-93-88854-05-4
Edition: 2019
Published by: Discovery Publishing House Pvt. Ltd., New Delhi (India)

Chapter 1

Empowerment of Women
A Socio-legal Study

[1]Dr. Puspanjali Padhal Retd. Principal
[2]Prof. Dr. Binayak Patnaik Director

Karjye Sumantri Karane Sudasi
Bhojye Sumata Shayane Surambha
Dharmanukula Kshmaya Dharitri

This is the portrayal of a woman's character enriched with variegated roles in her life in Ram-Gita.

According to Vedas both Stree Dharma and Purusha Dharma stand on equal footing. Male and female had mutual respect, co-operation and understanding. Indian womanhood was valued as somewhat sacred and sacrosanct.

Slowly and gradually devaluation of human values occurred. Our glorious culture faded away. It became pivotal in degrading the importance of a woman in the society. Discrimination between a man and a woman became rampant both in the family and in the society at large. It made the woman subject to torture physically, mentally, financially, emotionally, morally, psychologically and spiritually Even now, a son is preferred to a daughter and the later is considered as a burden to the family.

As a result, crime against women are rising high as waves in a tsunami. Laws are made. Punishments are shown stringent. But at last victim does not get justice. The wrongdoer gets escaped. This is the order of the day in spite of strict and arduous steps taken by the government.

[1] Govt. Women's College, Aska (Ganjam) Odisha.
[2] Shri Vaishnav Institute of Law, Indore (M.P.)

It seems the society has forgotten the fact that both woman and man are created by God. Society will run smoothly if it runs with the happy movement of both. So both should be treated as equal partners and both should be provided with equal opportunity. The country will make progress when both will participate in the developmental programmes and contribute their best.

It is felt that our society forgets the constitution of our country which contains several provisions for the well-being of all the citizens. It provides equal rights and opportunities for all. It never contains a single provision or the article which stands for partiality or gender bias. It is made on a wholesome thought and approach for creating a sound and healthy atmosphere in the vast arena of the society.

Man is a social animal. It is a truth and we all experience it in life when we want to lead a normal life. Society exists due to its individuals who are both male and female. Its survival works with the network of interdependence which nobody can deny. Man cannot live in isolation. One has to be social in order to live happily and comfortably with a sense of security. And this is the unwritten law of the universe.

We appear to ignore the social norms and discriminate women, naming them as the 'second sex'. They are marginalized and suffer from womb to tomb. Regret to mention the long list of sufferings they undergo like female feticide, dowry torture, bride burning, domestic violence, immoral trafficking, indecent representation, rape, child marriage, child labour, poor nutrition and ignorance shown to pregnant mothers, non-availability of ambulance during delivery, high infantile and maternal mortality, sexual harassment in the time of journey, in the workplace, ignominious status due to inequal wages and salary for doing equal work and many more.

The words "Empowerment of Women" have become a beautiful slogan in all the rallies and meetings. In reality, it seems as a showcase of powerful persons in the field of administration, politics and religion to achieve their ends in their lives. It is exemplified in the statement of an eminent minister of our country, who on the occasion of Women's

Day compared women with the cars and the houses with the garages. This is spoken before all the members of National Women's Association, MLA's and women entrepreneurs. It is an unscrupulous statement to say that if women will stay in the house they will not face any awkward situation as a car does not have any risk of accident as long as it is kept in the garage.

Another inhuman and unjudicious statement made by a senior administrator of one of the states of India may make us ashamed. When the villagers told they could not make toilets as they did not get money in the said scheme–The hateful and insulting quick retort of the officer was - "You may sell your wives and make your toilet ready".

These two examples are more than enough to reflect the way the women of India are treated.

According to a scientific report a female new born baby is a fighter than a male new born baby at the time of birth. There are more chances of survival for a physically poor baby girl than a physically poor baby boy just after birth. A woman is made sound than a man in this beautiful creation. But man wants to dominate her in various ways so that she cannot get chance to oppose the violence and torture. Thereby she is deprived of expressing her own desire and personality. Thus a woman is raped forcefully and oftentimes sexually exploited with terrible threats.

No doubt women enjoy voting rights. Even then society has a conservative attitude towards women. And we all know after years of struggle women in the Western world got their right to vote. Yet male chauvinism is perceived in all the nook and corner of the world. Some brave women-have come forward to fight against the ills and odds that come on their way.

The widows and divorcees lead a life of oppression and suppression. They are looked down upon as poor, lonely and ostracized human beings having no entity of their own. Society ill-treats them which is sheer injustice. They accept physical and mental abuse as a pattern of their lives. Their children are not looked after well and some of them become criminals at last. Thus our country loses the productivity of some section of the society which is certainly a social loss.

All widows and divorcees suffer in one way or the other. This is a social evil. They are forced to live in inhuman conditions. The widows are called as "shadowy women in white" after the death of their husbands. Women who are divorced for no fault of theirs are called destitutes. Thousands of widows spend their lives without any hope in the temple town of Vrindaban and the temple city of Varanasi. They beg and sing 'bhajans' for a single meal. They lead a dejected life sans freedom. In order to deprive the rich widows from their share of property, the family members leave them in such 'Ashrama' like places.

Even now a woman's life is dominated by her husband and in-laws. It is as if an evil if she ever tries to think and help her own parents. In spite of some progress seen in the social sphere, male domination exists in the name of custom, tradition and culture.

In this perspective we all women of our country should have knowledge on our constitution which provides steps for all kinds of our security. Illiteracy and ignorance are the social evils which should be removed drastically. As a result, each and every woman can have the knowledge to understand what is constitution, human rights and equal opportunities for all. At least all must know the constitutional provisions for the empowerment of women which are as follows:

Constitutional Provisions

- Article 12(2): No citizen std be discriminated in respect of any employment under the state only on the ground of sex.
- Article 14 : Right to equality before the law, which is applicable to both man and woman as a fundamental right.
- Article 15(3): Empowers the State to make special provisions for protection of women and children.
- Article 23 & 24 : Guarantees the right against exploitation which *inter alia* prohibits? Trafficking in human beings.

- Article 25(2)(*b*) : Mandates that the social reform and welfare can be provided irrespective of the right to freedom of religion.
- Article 39(*a*): Directs the State to secure the right to adequate means of livelihood to both men and women.
- Article 39(*d*): Directs the State to secure equal pay for equal work both for men and women.
- Article 42 : Directs the State to provide for just and humane condition of work and maternity relief.
- Article 44 : Directs the State to secure for the citizens an Uniform Civil Code throughout the territory of India.
- Article 51-A: Imposes certain fundamental duties on citizens which *inter alia* provides that every citizen is duty bound to renounce practices derogatory to the dignity of women.
- Articles 243-D and 243-T : Provides for reservation of one third seats for women in the Panchayats and Municipality respectively.
- Article 45 : Provides for early childhood care.
- Article 47: Stipulates the duty of the State to raise the level of nutrition and standard of living and improve public health.
- Article 24: Prohibits employment of children below 14 years in hazardous employment.
- Article 243-T (4) provides reservation of offices of Chairperson in Municipalities for SC, ST women according to State Legislative.

The society should honor the provisions of the constitution which is the heart and mind of India. Several legislative enactments have been framed to protect and safeguard the interests of women which get hindered during implementation. Government becomes serious and takes drastic measures which are visible in the enhancement of maternity leave, increase of seats for women in IITs and IIMs, amelioration programmes for widows and their children to bring them to the mainstream, steps to promote the all-round status of divorcees, tax benefits, incentives in case of the birth of baby girls, severe and immediate steps in case of domestic violence, rape and murder, sexual harassment cells in workplace and the recent historic decision of Supreme Court to end the system of Triple Talaqu for Muslim women and the like.

It appears plethora of laws are in vain only due to poor implementation. It is because the common man is not aware of the significance of these laws in their life. As a result, still discrimination on gender bias, domestic violence, rape and murder, dowry torture, bride burning, acid attack, female feticide, forced prostitution, destitution of widows and divorcees continue. Women fear to assert their rights if at all they know a little about their constitutional rights.

What to tell of the village women, even the educated women are afraid of going against the wrong doer and never come forward to file an FIR. It means they are yet to be made aware of their rights to live as human beings. They should be made conscious of the laws framed to protect them. In this regard, not only the family but also the society should extend to them help and co-operation.

In this perspective some Supreme Court Judgments should be cited in order to make our society aware of the rights of Women.

As per the United Nations Report 1980, "Women constitute half of the world population, perform nearly two-third of work hours, receive one-tenth of the world's, income and own less than one hundred percent of world's property".

The following are some judicial decisions in this regard:

- The disparity, which was prevalent in Hindu female's right to property is settled in the case of Thota Sesharathamma 1991.
- The Supreme Court in the case of Dr. Vijaya Monahar Arbat Vrs. Kasirao Rajaram Sawai and another, AIR 1987, S.C. 1100 decided that it is the duty of a son or a daughter to maintain their parents if they are not in a position to maintain themselves. It is also their duty

to look after their parents when they become old and infirm. If there are two or more children the parents may seek the remedy against any one or more of them.

- Prativa Rani Vrs. Suraj Kumar, AIR 1985, S.C. 628 is a landmark judgment with regard to the right of woman to her stridhana.
- A married daughter is allowed accommodation in parents' house as decided in the case of Savita Samvedi, SCR 1996.
- Adequate safeguards to working women against sexual harassment are provided in the case of Vishakha Vrs. State of Rajasthan, AIR 1997, S.C. 3011.
- The demand for dowry is considered as cruelty to woman as decided in the case of Sobharani Vrs. Madhukar, AIR 1988, S.C. 121.
- In the case of C. B. Muthamma V. Union of India, AIR 1979 S.C. 1868, the Supreme Court declared a rule as unconstitutional which stipulated the marriage as a disability for appointment to foreign service.
- In the case of M.A. Khan Vs. Shahabanu, AIR 1985 S.C. 945 the Supreme Court granted equal right to maintenance under Section 125 of the Criminal Procedure Code, 1973 to a divorced Muslim Woman notwithstanding the personal law.
- There are innumerable Supreme Court cases in India which reflect that the court has responded positively in protecting the rights of women and provide justice to them.
- In the very important judgment of AIR India V. Nargesh Meerza, AIR 1981, S.C. 1829 the Supreme Court considered the Air India Regulation as *Ultra vires* of Article-14 and 16(1) of the Constitution where pregnancy was considered as disqualification for that job.
- The S.C. in the case of State of Punjab Vrs. Amarjit Singh accepted dying declaration in case of dowry death even though police not recorded the same.

- The S.C. In the case of Delhi Domestic Working Women's Forum Vrs. Union of India (1995) suggested formulation of a scheme for awarding compensation to rape victims. The court suggested that the Criminals Injury Compensation Board or the Court should award compensation to the victims by taking into account the pain, suffering and shock as well as loss of earnings due to pregnancy and expenses of child birth if this occurred as the result of rape.
- In Anuj Garg Vs. Hotel Association of India, AIR 2005 SC 663 the SC held that Section 30 of Punjab Excise Act prohibiting women from employment in hotel and bars serving liquor violated gender equlity.
- In Maya Devi Vs. State of Maharashtra, ISCR (1986) p. 743 the requirement that a married woman should obtain her husband's consent before applying for public employment was held invalid and unconstitutional. It is an anachronistic obstacle to woman's equality.
- In Uttrakhand Mahila Parishad Vs. State of U.P., AIR 1992, SC 1965 unequal pay and less promotion avenues were deprecated.
- Right to privacy of women can not be invaded by any person as decided in the case of State of Maharashtra Vs. Madhuvan Mandikar, AIR 1991, SC 207.
- Guidelines are given for rescue and rehabilitation of the prostitutes to provide them to live with dignity as in the case of Gaurav Jain Vs. UOI, AIR 1997, SC 3021.

There are innumerable Supreme Court cases in India which reflect that the court has responded positively in protecting the rights of women and provide justice to them.

Women Empowerment and Law

The following laws are made which are helpful to protect the women and empower them as well:

- The Constitutional provisions in the Indian Constitution.

- The Pre-conception and Pre-natal Diagnostic Techniques (Prohibition of sex Selection) Act, 2002.
- The Pre-natal Diagnostic Techniques (Regulation and Prevention of Misuse). Act 1994.
- The Medical Termination of Pregnancy Act, 1971.
- The Medical Termination of Pregnancy Amendment Act, 2002.
- Child Labour (Prohibition & Regulation) Act, 1986.
- Child Marriage Restraint Act, 1929.
- Dowry Prohibition Act, 1961.
- Protection of Women from Domestic Violence Act, 2005.
- Indecent Representation of Women (Prohibition) Act, 1986.
- Suppression of Immoral Trafficking of Women & Girls Act, 1956.
- Indian Penal Code, 1860.
- The Commission of Sati (Prevention) Act, 1987.
- Women under Maintenance under Section 125 Cr.P.C.
- Maternity Benefit Act, 1961.
- Equal Remuneration Act, 1976.
- Factories Act, 1984.
- Hindu Succession Act, 1956.
- Hindu Adoption & Maintenance Act, 1956.
- Hindu minority and Guardianship Act, 1956.
- Family Courts Act, 1948.
- The National Commission for Women Act, 1990.

Laws for Working Women

Several laws are made for working women which are as follows:

- Equal Remuneration Act, 1976 provides equal remuneration for the same work or a work of similar nature and for the prevention of discrimination on the basis of sex.

- Maternity Benefit Act, 1961 regulates the employment of women in certain establishment for certain periods before and after child birth and to provide for maternity benefit and certain other benefits.
- Female daily wagers are entitled to maternity benefit as decided in the Supreme Court case of Municipal Corp. of Delhi Vrs. Female Workers (Muster roll).
- Establishment means a factory, a mine, a plantation, shop, an establishment where in persons are employed for the execution of equestrian, acrobatic and other performances, etc.
- Factories Act, 1984 prescribes provisions for protection of women workers such as separate latrines, urinals, washing facilities and provisions of creches.
- Employees Provident Fund Family Pension Linked and deposit Insurance Fund Act, 1952 prescribes that the widow is entitled for family pension.
- The sexual harassment of women at work place (Prevention, Prohibition, Redressal) Act, 2013, included employment in a house and in any dwelling place.
- Sexual harassment violates fundamental rights of women under articles 14, 15 and 21 which includes living with dignity and the right to women to work in a safe environment.

All over the globe efforts are on to eradicate the evil of inequality among men and women. It is reflected in the field of arts, film, literature and theatre. People have become conscious. Revolution has already started from the village level. Yet village women are afraid of the society when they want to break the barriers of unwritten laws.

The following lines depict the agony of women due to unequal treatment in the society.

"I am the woman who holds up the sky
The rainbow nuns through my eyes
The sun makes a path to my wombs
My thoughts are in the shape of clouds
But my words are yet to come."

A female MP in Australia struggled no doubt, but could take part in the activity of the Parliament and delivered her speech in a standing position while breast feeding her baby. An Australian athlete and a runner could make forty marathons alone in forty days by the side of forty rivers of forty countries. It was a part of her awareness programme to save river water from pollution. Aparna Kumar, an IPS officer of India could climb 'Denali' - the highest mountain of America after getting success in climbing Mount Everest in 2016. They are certainly great achievers- symbolic representatives of womenhood.

When the Electricity Board denied to pay compensation to the husband of the deceased wife Malati in Puducherry, depicting her a mere housewife who fell a victim to the electric wire fallen in the field, the Madras High Court compelled the Board to give compensation. Court said she was not to be ignored as a housewife with no earning. It said in the decision - she was not only the home maker but also a dutiful wife, a beloved mother of two children, the finance minister and chartered accountant of her home as well.

In one decision Supreme Court Justice, A.K. Sikri appealed to the people that court is there to give the right decision but the whole of the society has to change its mindset. His was the emotional statement-if husbands cannot make wives better halves, at least they can make them equal halves. It was also stated - right to women to have pregnancy must be there - it is not the right of the husband or in-laws to decide.

Good news comes from Northern India in the form of extending co-operation towards women when a bride goes in 'Barat to Bridegroom's house, gets married and both return to bride's home to stay. The bridegroom accepts the surname of the bride magnanimously. This is no doubt, a welcome step for the change of the society to liberate women from male domination and patriarchy.

Vivekananda rightly said that without emancipation of womanhood the progress of the world is impossible. It will remain a myth if half of the section of the society is ignored, underestimated and uncared for. It is just like a bird fails to fly in the sky with the help of one wing.

In July 2017, there was a congregation of women leaders of three states of India- Madhya Pradesh, Rajasthan and Chhatisgarh. It was "Bama Triveni Sammelana working for empowering women. Dr. Santos from Udaipur, Dr. Aruna Shrivastava, Professor in Law from Bhopal, Nita and others opined that instead of right to equality women suffer from home to workplace. Regret to inform, they told, even today the society hesitates to take opinions and decisions of women in social and religious fields. Still debacle is created on their way though they struggle hard to go ahead in all walks of life.

The judicial decision on 'Triple Talaq' is a welcome step to free Muslim Women from a life of fear and submission.

Whatever is achieved in this regard we all have to admit the help and co-operation of men who believe that a woman is the source of strength in every walk of life.

The following suggestions may be taken into consideration for the protection and empowerment of women:

- Implementation of the universal declaration of human rights in realistic terms.
- Participation of every man and woman for protection of human rights which is a constant struggle.
- Human Rights Cell for registration of the cases of violation of human rights and education to the people about the human rights.
- Human Rights Enforcement machinery for enforcement of human rights.
- Human Rights Training for paramilitary force and police to stop misuse of human rights.
- Human Rights clause and enforcement of the same are to be incorporated in the Constitution of India along with human duties.
- Human Rights awareness to the people by electronic and printed media.

- Processions for protection of human rights are required to be taken out occasionally.
- Human Rights Groups are to be formulated in Schools, Colleges and Universities to educate them about human rights.
- Human Rights Talk Programme are required to made and organised.
- Human Rights institutions and organsiations like G.O. and N.G.O. are required to be made in each State to look after the violation and maintenance of human rights.
- Celebration of human rights day in every year.
- All acts, customs and regulation that go against the human rights should be discontinued.
- The legislation, judicial decisions and administrative arrangement should be under constant review for promotion of human rights.
- Separate curriculum for human rights.
- Rape and other human violation by paramilitary forces and police must be stopped during search and seize.
- Rape in police custody should be stopped.
- Illicit treatment of women in Jail should be stopped.
- Female foeticide caused by ultra sound before the birth should be stopped.
- Community groups should be set up to provide loan funds for the women.
- Women should be allowed to give advice and take decision along with the husband and other male members in domestic matters.
- Special Women Human Right Forum is required to be formulated.
- Special programme are to be made in remote, rural, tribal areas and for backward classes to give education to them that girls must be educated.
- Wife beating and character assassination of the woman should be stopped. Everything should be settled mutually.

If that fails then there should be judicial separation till the understanding is made, if that fails then the decree of divorce should be made.

- Non adoption of female child is against human rights of woman.
- Politically there must be 50% representation of women in the parliament.
- Equal wages for equal works for women. Special mechanism should be made to look after this in unorganised and private sectors.
- Females need to be given training so as to improve their physical power as they are also equally competent for this.
- There must be mutual respect, understanding between husband and wife.
- In Hindu Community the disrespected part of the Karva Chouth which is against human rights should be changed with the sanction of Saints and Sadhus.
- Poverty, illiteracy, ignorance and population growth are the root causes of various problems which also in cludes the problems of health of women. Therefore strong steps should be taken to eliminate all these causes.
- Violence in the family (sexual abuse, dowry, rape, marital rape, battering, etc.), violence in the community (rape, sexual harassment at work place and educational institution, trafficking), violence by the State (custodial torture and rape) should be stopped to protect the health of women.
- The domestic violence of any form against women should be stopped by appropriate mechanism as women cannot expose violence due to prestige.
- The purdah and dowry system are to be eradicated, which are against human rights.

- In Muslim community the husband and the wife relation should be a matter of compromise and balance. For this a uniform civil code is necessary.
- Women recreation centres are required for the service holders.
- More nos. of family courts are required for settlement of family disputes.
- Awareness programmes should be made regarding health of women.
- Public Interest Litigation (PIL) is an effective instrument to root out all problems which also includes the problem of health of woman.
- A conscious and conscientious approach is necessary to protect the health of the women besides legislative enactments, judicial decisions, administrative orders, role of commissions, committees, Govt. and Non-Govt. Organisations and conventions.

All of us should hope for the best. We should try to free ourselves from the tradition-bound superstitious mindset to change our hearts and minds so that women can live in the society with equal social dignity. They can be great artists, selfless social workers, able administrators, good doctors, accountable engineers, renowned teachers and great mothers of healthy children who will really shoulder the responsibility of protecting as well as enhancing the glory of our independent nation.

"O Lord why have you not given woman the right to conquer her destiny, why does she have to wait head bowed, by the roadside, waiting with tired patience, hoping for a miracle in the morrow?"

—Rabindra Nath Tagore

Human Rights Management after Globalization **Pages 16-24**
Edited by: Dr. Rabi Narayana Misra
ISBN: 978-93-88854-05-4
Edition: 2019
Published by: Discovery Publishing House Pvt. Ltd., New Delhi (India)

Chapter 2

Globalization and its Impact on Human Rights

[1]Roopesh Kumar Misra
[2]N. Rajasekhar Rao

Introduction

The word 'globalization' is now used widely to sum up todays world order. It means they increasingly integrate the world into one capitalist political economy operating under a neo-liberal free market ideology. Economic globalization as witnessed in the world today is not a new phenomenon. It has been evolving for the past several years and gaining momentum day by day. The trend, at present, is a shift from a world economy based on national market economies to a borderless global market economy increasingly governed by one set of rules. In this context, globalization means global economic liberalization, developing a global financial system and a transnational production system which is based on a homogenized worldwide law of value[3]. The demise of the Cold War helped the emergence of a new aggressive "competitive global economic order. This was possible mainly due to the integration of the newly industrialized countries and much of the developing nations. Although globalization and market liberalization have made some progress in terms of economic growth in certain countries, it has also had many negative impacts in developing societies.

Global Activities

Richard Barnet of the Institute of Policy Studies describes globalization in terms of four increasing webs of global

[1] MBA, MCA, M.Tech., Manager Mumbai
[2] Government Degree College Ravulapalem, Andhra Pradesh

commercial activity: *global cultural bazaar, the global shopping mall; the global financial network; the global workplace.* The global cultural bazaar promotes the notion of uniform cultural values and products across the world. This idea influenced billions of people, shaping their goals and homogenizing their tastes and attitudes towards a desired fantasy lifestyle. The unprecedented increase in global trade—the buying and selling of goods and services among countries—has created a planetary supermarket. The cultural bazaar and shopping mall intersect through the vehicle of advertising. Media has become a powerful player in the globalization process. In fact, globalization of economies has also led to the globalization of media. Media is used to impose the culture and power of the wealthy nations from the global North. The global financial market has created a new atmosphere to search for quick profits. The foreign exchange market is mainly dealing with currency speculation, bet for or against foreign currencies. The increasing mobility of jobs has created global workplaces and this has boosted international labour migration. In other words, the globalization and market-oriented economic reforms helped transnational companies shift their manufacturing units to developing countries. Because of this more people are crossing borders in search of jobs and in most conditions people are forced to work in inhuman conditions for lower wages. All these proved the fact that globalization is not a simple but a very complex set of process that operates at multiple levels—political, economic and cultural. Nicaraguan scholar Xabier Gorostiaga argues that in this era of globalization humanity is perceived as fundamentally one, with a common destiny that is the result of a technological revolution in information and communication and the awareness of the un sustainability of the current way of life.

In an article titled "The Human Rights Debate in an Era of Globalization: Hegemoney of Discourse", Nikhil Aziz describes two kinds of globalization based on Richard Falks theory on the making of Global Citizenship. He argues that we can see globalization in different perspectives: Globablization from Above (GA) and Globalization from Below (GB). At the political level, GA manifests itself in its action of the Western countries, particularly the United States of America and global financial institutions in pressuring countries of the South to democratize. This translates as the adoption of a Western-style liberal democratic system of governance. They closely tie economic Globalization from Above to the political aspect in that (1) the source of pressure for change is the same, and (2) close links are alleged between the ideologies of free markets and free societies. Economic Globalization from Above entails countries of the South to accept - within the parameters of the dominant World capitalist system - the imposition of structural adjustment programmes, neo-liberal economic policies, including the wholesalc liberalization of domestic economies, to allow unrestricted entry to transnational capital. On a cultural level, GA arises from the control of the global information and communication networks by Western media corporations; and the spread of modern technologies of a consumerist culture, and Western cultural expressions as the global culture.

The transnational companies are the spearheads of globalization and have become the dominant economic and political force in the world economy. Increasing competition and pressure on transnational companies to increase profits leads to a relentless search for cheap labour markets. Many of the companies from the developed and the Newly Industrialized Countries (NIC) have shifted their manufacturing and service industries to developing countries. For example, several major airlines now have their global accounting done in India. A large number of computer software companies from the United States are developing software in Bangalore, India, at less than one-fifth of the price in other countries. The German car manufacturing company BMW and Lorean car manufacturers like Daewoo and Hyundai have already established their manufacturing units in Vietnam. The Export Processing Zones of many developing countries are catering to the needs of the transnational companies by way of providing cheap labour. The International Labour Resource and Information Group based at the University of Cape Town has described these phenomena a race downhill in which countries underbid each other.

Because they cannot see an alternative, workers also end up underbidding one another. The main arguments are competitiveness and the need to survive. But for workers it is a race to the bottom and the bottom means slave like conditions. When work moves to less developed countries, the shift does not automatically bring Western levels of employment and prosperity to the host countries. What it does bring are very profitable high-tech islands and Export processing Zones where they protect transnational capital, with the help of the state, from social responsibility.

There may be short-term advances in the living standards of a small group of workers. Nevertheless, when some workers elsewhere lead the race to the bottom, those jobs may disappear. A report by UNCTAD notes that transnational companies encroach on areas over which sovereign responsibilities have traditionally been reserved for national governments. A situation has arisen where many goverments of developing countries no longer control the flow of financial capital; so they can no longer control their own economies.

Globalization has substantially contributed to the intensification of debt, poverty and economic crisis in the developing world. The Structural Adjustment Programmes (SAP) designed and imposed by the global creditor institutions is a typical instrument to create a favourable atmosphere for globalization, which ultimately affects developing countries. In order to meet the mandates set by the SAP, a country spends less by cutting back government expenditures, social services, and economic investments so that resources can be placed elsewhere. More money is being spent on export orientation, which results in local economies becoming dependent on the integration with the world economy. The international lenders demand poor economies to divert substantial resources away from sectors serving domestic needs: withdraw all subsidies for poor people, privatize the state sector, deregulate the market and decrease wages. In effect, this process opens up countries to globalization. Thus structural adjustment programmes and import-export-led strategies of industralization were part of a political and economic restructuring process, a prelude to globalization. The advocates of globalization give philosophical justifications to accept export-led growth, lower wages and living standards for workers, shrinking government budgets, and extremely high interest rates. They say "There Is No Alternative" - TINA, the phrase coined by British Prime Minister Margaret Thatcher in 1980s. Powerful institutions like the International Monetary Fund, the World Bank and the World Trade Organization raise the TINA, argument to persuade the developing nations to qualify themselves to borrow money. The developing countries are left into no option but to accept the liberalization and market-oriented reforms. Under this liberalization policy production tends to be export-oriented. Meeting the basic needs of the people becomes less important. State-run factories or enterprises are often privatized to suit the needs of foreign investors. Free trade and liberalization lead to competition and local producers, like farmers, have to suffer the consequences.

Globalization has created a situation where the role and importance of nation-state is becoming irrelevant. Kenichi Ohmae, widely recognized as one of todays top business gurus, asks, in a world where economic borders are disappearing and money flows around the globe beyond the reach of governments, "who, indeed needs the nation-state?" He argues that 4 Is-Investment, Industry, Information technology and Individual consumers-make the traditional middleman function of nation-states and of their governments, largely unnecessary. Because, the global markets for all the Is work just fine on their own, nation-states no longer have to play a market-making role. In this situation multinational corporations are becoming the actors even in international politics. A growing trend to promote the idea of recapturing the capitalist frontier and its lost values is more visible through the globalization and market liberalization in the developing countries. It is true that a few rich or middle class people have emerged in societies where transition to market system has been introduced. China and Vietnam are typical examples. In these countries a newly rich class has emerged as a result of gloablization and market reforms. Several other Asian countries are also witnessing the emergence of a few rich and middle class people at the expenses of many poor. These new-rich and middle class are really the products of globalization and they provide the market for imported products and further strengthening the economy of the developed countries. While analyzing the economic development, social status and political consciousness of the new-rich in Asia, Richard Robinson and David S. G. Goodman observe that it is as consumers that the new-rich of Asia have attracted an interest of almost cargo-cult proportions in the West. They constitute the new markets for Western products: processed foods, computer software, educational services and films and television soaps. They are the new tourists, bringing foreign exchange in hard times. What has helped such an enthusiastic embrace of the Asian new-rich is that they are emerging at a time when prolonged recession and low growth rates have depressed home markets in the West. The emergence of the new middle class and their wealth manifest themselves in the society in several ways. This is more visible through a new emerging culture which Robinson and Goodman describe as Mobile phones, McDonalds and middle-class revolution. It is estimated that 55,000 people a day regularly pass through the McDonalds restaurant in central Beijing - (Chinas first, opened in 1992) - to pay for a hamburger much more than the most Chinese will earn in a fortnight. It was reported that in 1993 a mobile telephone number 58888 containing four lucky eights – was auctioned for 1,30,000 RMB. An ordinary mobile phone itself costs about 25,000 RMB in China to buy, install and register, and there are monthly service and user fees to pay. This McDonald and Mobile phone culture has already spread among the new-rich in many developing countries because of the globalization of markets. Even Cambodia and Bangladesh the world's most poverty stricken countries, are affected. A globalization of taste has occurred in every field of the developing world. Consumer goods like Levis Jeans, Nike athletic shoes, and Herme's scarves are visible all over the world now. A decade ago Kenichi Ohmae described this process, driven by global exposure to the same information, the same cultural icons, and the same advertisements, as the "Californiazation" of taste. He now argues that, today, however, the process of convergence goes faster and deeper. It reaches well beyond taste to much more fundamental dimensions of world-view, mind-set. There are now, for example, tens of millions of teenagers around the world who, having been raised in a multimedia-rich environment, have a lot more in common with each other than they do with members of older generations in their own cultures. Well, one group is considering this an achievement of globalization. On the other hand, the reality is that, "globalization requires the humiliation of hundreds of millions of people keeping them in constant insecurity, pitting them against one another in a competitive struggle for survival". The Human Development Report of 1997 says; Globalization can also shift patterns of consumption. Luxury cars and soft drinks can rapidly become a part of daily life, heightening relative deprivation. The pattern can increase absolute poverty by undermining the production of goods on which poor people rely. A flood of imported wheat can shift consumption away from sorghum or cassava, making them scarcer in loval markets.

Roberto Verzola, a social activist of the Philippines, comments that in the same way that colonization was the trend one hundred years ago, globalization is, today. Today global corporations have replaced the colonial powers. In developing countries, global corporations are allowed to feast on natural resources, human resources, and national wealth, they displace farmers from their land, workers from their jobs, and communities from their roots. They are responsible for the breaking up of communities and the destruction of the environment to serve the human and raw material requirements of global production for the global market. The consequence is the collapse of food security and the emergence of global environmental crises, which in the end may turn out to be even worse than colonization. Even the peoples of developed countries suffer from the profit-hungry rules of global corporations today, which virtually rule the world. Globalization and market-oriented economic reforms have been designed for the benefit of these groups. In reality, globalization means the rule of global corporations. It means decision about lives are being made in corporate boardrooms in the USA, Europe and Japan, instead of in local community councils or at the national level. National governments are becoming the implementors of orders received from the international actors. This has created a situation of powerlessness and suffering for many in developing countries which results in violation of rights of millions of people.

Globalization, Development and Human Rights

The relation between globalization, development and human rights raises policy and legal questions. One such question is whether globalization of market-oriented economic system is essential for development and protection of human rights? While searching for an answer to this question we should analyze how we perceive the concept of development and human rights, especially in the context of developing countries. Human rights have become an integral part of the process of globalization in many ways. The Western countries are increasingly using their view of human rights concept as a yardstick to judge developing countries and to deal with economic and trade relations to extend development assistance. At the same time globalization intensifies impoverishment by increasing the poverty, insecurity, fragmentation of society and thus violates human rights and human dignity of millions of people.

Development or economic development is widely perceived as a historical process that takes place in almost all societies characterized by economic growth and increased production and consumption of goods and services. Development is also often used in a normative sense as a multi-valued social goal covering such diverse spheres as better material well-being, living standards, education, health care, wider opportunities for work and leisure and in essence the whole gamut of desirable social and material welfare. But, in todays globalization, the concept of development itself is interpreted differently and the concept of right to development is not taken seriously.

Conclusion

The Preamble of the Declaration of the Right to Development, adopted by the UN General Assembly in 1986, describes "development as a comprehensive economic, social, cultural and political process that aims at the constant improvement of the well-being of the entire population and of all individuals on the basis of their active, free and meaningful participation in development and in the fair distribution of resulting benefits". The 1990 UN Global Consultation on the Right to Development as a Human Right, stated that the right to development is an inalienable human right with the human being as the central subject to the right and that all the aspects of the right to development set forth in the Declaration of the Right to Development are indivisible and interdependent, and these include civil, political, economic, social, and cultural rights. It was further maintained that the right to development is the right of individuals, groups and peoples to participate in, contribute to, and enjoy continuous economic, social, cultural and political development, in which all human rights and fundamental freedoms can be fully realized. A development strategy that disregards or interferes with human rights is the very negation of development.

The aims and objectives of the so-called development models promoted by different governments or international development agencies are not compatible with human rights standards. A new model of development ideology is being promoted that is based on the market and its logic. Several decades of discussion on alternative development model is withering away and a dominant model of market-oriented development taking roots in that place. As a result of the globalization process, more negative effects are visible now. Global integration of the structures, processes, and ideologies produce injustice, oppression, exploitation and maldevelopment in society. The systematic integration of the forces that are dominant in the globalization process intensifies human rights violations.

Human Rights Management after Globalization **Pages 25-31**
Edited by: Dr. Rabi Narayana Misra
ISBN: 978-93-88854-05-4
Edition: 2019
Published by: Discovery Publishing House Pvt. Ltd., New Delhi (India)

Chapter 3

Critical Evaluation of Children Rights in India

[1]Dr. (Prof.) R.P. Sharma
[2]Dr. Mukku Syam Babu

Introduction

India is a young nation; census 20 U had counted more than 440 million children in India below 18 years of age constituting 37 per cent of the total population of the country. Within the age group of 0-17 years, children between 0-6 years constituted about 14 per cent of the total population of children in India followed by 17 per cent between 7-14 years and the remaining 6 per cent in the age group of 15-17 years. In India, a huge chunk of the child population is vulnerable at birth till they attain self-sustaining capabilities, physically, emotionally and mentally. They would require the optimum handholding of the adults to reach that stage of self-sustaining capabilities. They are vulnerable and hence are always at risk against the vagaries of the world, be it natural (e.g. calamities) or manmade (e.g. war, unrest etc.).

The Indian government initiated endeavor through different policies, legislative Acts, National Plan of Action, schemes and programs for protection of Children rights. These legal Acts, schemes and programs though are part of the concerted efforts of the government to protect the well-being of children of this country but perhaps not yet enough to mitigate the rising cases of all types of exploitation meted out to children.

[1] Prof. of Economics (Rtd.) Berhampur-10, Odisha
[2] M. Com., M.Phil., Ph.D., Government Degree College, Razole East Godavari Dt. AP

The Constitution of India provides that the State shall direct its policy towards ensuring "*that children are given opportunities and facilities to develop in a healthy manner and in conditions of freedom and dignity and that childhood and youth are protected against exploitation and against moral and material abandonment*". This directive clearly positions children as deserving of the highest priority in national realisation of the Fundamental Rights and the special provisions for those most vulnerable to discrimination and exclusion. This is India's clear national mandate for what must be done, through policy, law, planning, and practical programming, with conscious provision of the required resources of knowledge and skills, time and attention, material and financial support, and dedicated practical effort to reach all children, throughout the period of childhood. The National Policy for Children reaffirms this as a pledge to every child.

Human Rights to Children

There are four broad classifications of human rights that should be afforded to children. These four categories cover all civil, political, social, economic and cultural rights of every child:

- *Right to Survival:* A child's right to survival begins before a child is born. According to Government of India, a child life begins after twenty weeks of conception. Hence the right to survival is inclusive of the child rights to be born, right to minimum standards of food, shelter and clothing and the right to live with dignity.
- *Right to Protection:* A child has the right to be protected from neglect, exploitation and abuse at home, and elsewhere.
- *Right to Participation:* A child has a right to participate in any decision making that involves him/her directly or indirectly. There are varying degrees of participation as per the age and maturity of the child.
- *Right to Development:* Children have the right to all forms of development: Emotional, Mental and Physical. Emotional development is fulfilled by proper care and love of a support system, mental development through education and learning and physical development through recreation, play and nutrition.

According to the Integrated Child Protection Scheme (ICPS) Child Protection is about keeping children safe from a risk or perceived risk to their lives or childhood. It is about recognizing that children are vulnerable and hence reducing their vulnerability by protecting them from harm and harmful situations. Child protection is about ensuring that children have a security net to depend on and if they happen to fall through the holes in the system, the system has the responsibility to provide the child with the necessary care and rehabilitation to bring them back into the safety net.

CHILD PROTECTION

Prevention	Intervention	Rehabilitation
• Law and Policies	• Laws and Policies	• Laws and Policies
• Processes and Protocols	• Access and Assistance	• Long term care until age 18
• Mechanisms and Systems	• Immediate Relief (SOS attention)	• Skills and Training
• Monitoring	• Restoration of rights/ Status Quo	
• Sensitization and Awareness Building	• Punish violators	

Legal Framework

In 1974, the Government of India adopted a National Policy for Children, declaring the nation's children as 'supremely important assets'. The Department of Women and Child Development was set up in the Ministry of Human Resource Development in 1985. The Department implements several other programmes, undertakes advocacy and inter-sectoral monitoring catering to the needs of women and children. In pursuance of this, the Department formulated a National Plan of Action for Children in 1992. The Government of India ratified the Convention on the Rights of the Child on 12 November, 1992. By ratifying the Convention on the Rights of the Child, the Government is obligated "to review National and State legislation and bring it in line with provisions of the Convention". The Convention revalidates the rights guaranteed to children by the Constitution of India, and is, therefore, a powerful weapon to combat forces that deny these rights. India submitted its first/initial report to the Committee on the Rights of the Child in 1997. The purpose of this first report was to give the Committee a sense of the situation of children in India. The report outlines the various laws and policies pertaining to children that are being implemented in the country. The report outlines steps taken by India to fulfill the UNCRC commitments.

Government of India has adopted the Meena project to promote positive images of the girl child. Measures were taken to improve the Civil Registration System. Central Adoption and Resource Agency (CARA) was constituted to act as an information centre for children available for inter-country adoption and receiving adoption applications. The Govt. of India was said to be taking several measures to protect the rights of children with disabilities as per the provisions of the Persons with Disabilities (Equal Opportunities, Protection of Rights and Full Participation) Act, 1995. With regard to child health, the Government was taking initiatives to strengthen the existing Reproductive and Child Health Programmes. The Government of India gave special attention to children National Disaster Relief Plan to meet the needs of children in emergency situations including situations of conflict. With regard to sexual exploitation and abuse of children the government had many provisions to protect children in the Indian pejial code. India also has an emergency helpline for children: CHILDLINE 1098. The government had also amended the Immoral Traffic (Prevention) Act, 1956 to counter trafficking of children.

A list of Acts & Laws for Child Protection

Below is a comprehensive list of Acts and other laws of the land for the protection and care of the children in India:

- Protection of Children from Sexual Offences Act, 2012.
- Bonded Labour System (Abolition) Act, 1976.
- Children (Pledging of Labour) Act, 1933.
- Child Labour (Prohibition and Regulation) Rules, 1988.

- Child Labour (Prohibition and Regulation) Act, 1986.
- Commissions for Protection of Child Rights Rule, 2006.
- Commissions for Protection of Child Rights (Amendment) Act, 2006.
- Commissions for Protection of Child Rights Act, 2006.
- Convention on the Rights of Children CRC.
- Factories Act, 1948.
- Guardians and Wards Act, 1890.
- Hindu Minority Guardians Act, 1956.
- Immoral Traffic (Prevention) Act, 1956.
- Infant Milk Substitutes Feeding Bottles and Infant (regulation of Production, Supply and Distribution) Amendment Act, 2003.
- Juvenile Justice (Care and Protection of Children) Act, 2015.
- Prohibition of Child Marriage Act, 2006.
- Right of Children to Free and Compulsory Education Act, 2009.
- Young Persons (Harmful Publication) Act, 1956.

The National Policy for Children, 2013: The National Policy for Children, 2013 was adopted by the Government on 26th April, 2013. It adheres to the Constitutional mandate and guiding principles of UN CRC and reflects a paradigm shift from a "need-based" to a "rights-based" approach. It emphasises that the State is committed to take affirmative measures to promote equal opportunities for all children, and to enable all children in its jurisdiction to exercise all the constitutional rights. The National Policy for Children, 2013 recognizes that:

- A child is any person below the age of eighteen years;
- Childhood is an integral part of life with a value of its own;
- Children are not a homogenous group and their different needs need different responses, especially the multi dimensional vulnerabilities experienced by children in different circumstances;

- A long term, sustainable, multi-sectoral, integrated and inclusive approach is necessary for the overall and harmonious development and protection of children.

The Present Situation

The situation related poverty, water, sanitation and health shows extremely dismal picture, even after almost seven decades of independence of India. There are close to two million homeless in the country and the larger states share the burden of the homeless more than the relatively smaller states.

Right to development is described as the right of every child to education, play, leisure, cultural activities, access to information and freedom of thought, conscience and religion. While the 'education for all' is still elusive, the concept of play and leisure is elusive as well for a large section of children driven by poverty and forced to work and earn.

Domestic violence leaves long standing impact on the mental and emotional growth on the children. Men who have witnessed their parents' domestic violence are three times more likely to abuse their own wives than children of non-violent parents, with the sons of the most violent parents being 1000 times more likely to become wife beaters.

Right to Participation define the right of the children to be listened to, to freely express their views and to freedom of expression, though, association and access to information. The question often asked is if children can be burdened with housework, farm chores and income generation, why cannot they have the right to participate in decisionmaking process that affect their own lives.

To conclude, it may be mentioned that the Government of India has over the years brought progressive policies, legislations and programmes for the well being of children of India. The Integrated Child Development Scheme (ICDS) and Childline Service are two programmes that are the largest in the world which supports the development and protection of children in India. However, despite all the best efforts, the situation of children and child rights in India is grim and far beyond any satisfactory level. Poverty is the central issue that needs to be tackled. The well being of a child rests upon a child having a caring and protective family environment. Thus, nothing less than a consolidated and holistic approach towards integrating income generation, providing access to education, health services, access to safe ater and a healthy, protective environment is desirable. This can change the lives of the millions of children and ensure their rights for survival, protection, development and participation.

Human Rights Management after Globalization **Pages 32-43**
Edited by: Dr. Rabi Narayana Misra
ISBN: 978-93-88854-05-4
Edition: 2019
Published by: Discovery Publishing House Pvt. Ltd., New Delhi (India)

Chapter 4

Impact of Globalisation on Human Rights

An Overview

[1]Dr. S. Durga
[2]B. Ratnavalli

Introduction

Global development is sometimes viewed as being responsible for disenfranchisement, exploitation, and other forms of human rights abuses. On the other hand, improvements in human rights are sometimes attributed to the spread of liberal ideas, which is one of the key dimensions of globalization. On the one hand, many argue that economic integration in trade and investment generates incentives for governments to abuse poor and disenfranchised people, so that repression, exploitation and human rights abuses arise. Economic freedom refers to the internal liberalization of economic rights, such as the "freedom to engage in economic transactions, without government interference but with government support of the institutions necessary for that freedom, including rule of law, sound money, and open markets". Globalization is a multidimensional phenomenon, comprising "numerous complex and interrelated processes that have a dynamism of their own" (U.N., 2000). It involves a deepening and broadening of rapid trans boundary exchanges due to developments in technology, communications, and media (UN, 2001). Such exchanges and interactions occur at all levels of governance and among non-state actors, creating a more interdependent world. Human rights violations continue to be the norm rather than the exception.

1 Assistant Professors Department of Management Studies TJPS College, Guntur.
2 Assistant Professors, Department of Management Studies, TJPS College, Guntur.

Development poses challenges to international human rights law, because for the most part that law has been designed to restrain abuses by powerful states and state agents. While globalization has enhanced the ability of civil society to function across borders and promote human rights, other actors have gained the power to violate human rights in unforeseen ways. International human rights law aims primarily to protect individuals and groups from abusive action by states and state agents.

Globalization has resulted in informalization of labour. Only 8 per cent of the labour force in India is in the formal economy while 90 per cent work in the informal economy with no legal protection or security and are subject to ruthless exploitation. Many companies including TNCs (transnational companies) got rid of their unionized labour force and moved their operations to low wage and depressed areas to avail themselves of the large supply of unorganized and unprotected, mainly female labour. Mathews George Chunakara describes the state of workers in developing countries after globalization as a race to the bottom, and the bottom means slave like conditions. He explains this by the search of transnational companies for cheap labour in order to maximize their profits, so the governments of developing countries compete for the investors by providing cheaper labour.

In Asia, in particular, the migration of large numbers of female workers to the Middle East from. It has been estimated, for example, that the ratio of females to males who comprise migrant labour is 12:1 among Filipinos migrating to Asian destinations; 3:1 among Indonesians and 3:2 among Sri Lankans. Many of these women work as domestic workers, seamstresses, nurses, assistants in retail shops and restaurants, labour conditions and mechanisms of both social and physical security in receiving countries seem to be perilous at best. More often than not,receiving States tend not to observe even minimal labour standards with regard to migrant workers, particularly women. Heavy economic dependence of the sending States on the inward monetary remittances of migrant workers has inhibited them from demanding fair labour conditions and protection from receiving States, thereby further weakening the position of such workers. Women have entered the workforce in large numbers in States that have embraced liberal economic policies. One United Nations survey concludes that "it is by now considered a stylized fact that industrialization in the context of globalization is as much female-led as it is export led" According to the Women's Environment and Development Organization (WEDO) women bear the disproportionate weight of the constraints introduced under the yoke of globalization. All these massive development projects have been promoted by TNCs in collabouration with local governments.

International Response

In his report to the UN Millennium Summit, Kofi Annan, described the world of globalization, "... as a new context for and a new connectivity among economic actors and activities throughout the world. Globalization has been made possible by the progressive dismantling of barriers to trade and capital mobility, together with fundamental- technological advances and steadily declining costs of transportation, communication and computing. Its integrative logic seems inexorable, its momentum irresistible."

When globalization is interpreted as internationalization, the term refers to a growth of transactions and interdependence between countries. From this perspective, a more global world is one where more messages, ideas, merchandise, money, investments and people cross borders between national-state-territorial units. A second common analytical dead-end in discussions of globalization has equated the notion with liberalization. In this case, globalization denotes a process of removing officially imposed restrictions on movements of resources between countries in order to form an 'open' and 'borderless' world economy. On this understanding, globalization occurs as authorities reduce or abolish regulatory measures like trade barriers, foreign-exchange restrictions, capital controls and visa requirements.

The international protection of civil and political rights emerged later, becoming an aim of the international community at the end of World War II in response to the atrocities committed during that conflict. A number of U.N. specialized agencies have also addressed the question of globalization. The ILO has long tackled the phenomenon. From the Copenhagen Social Summit in 1995 to the 1998 Declaration on Fundamental Principles and Rights at Work, the ILO has pressed for an international consensus on the content of the core labour standards that provide a social floor to the global economy. In 1998, the ILO adopted the Convention concerning the Prohibition and Immediate Action for the Elimination of the Worst Forms of Child Labour. It also adopted its Declaration on Fundamental Principles and Rights at Work together with a follow-up procedure based upon technical cooperation and reporting. The principles have been incorporated into codes of conduct by the private sector and also used as a basis for action by various regional communities sought to include good governance in public affairs, democracy, respect for human rights, and respect for the rule of law, essential in the elements of the accord, with the termination of assistance for non-respect of any of the elements. Jurists are analysing the issue whether globalization impacts on the implementation of human rights as stated in the Universal Declaration of Human Rights (1948) and the subsequent United Nations agreements, particularly the covenant on civil and political rights (1966), the covenant on economic, social and cultural rights (1966) and the declaration on the right to development (1986). They often relate one aspect of human rights to the other aspect of globalization for instance relating poverty in developing countries to debt or relating unemployment to privatization, or relating health deterioration to the monopoly of medicine patents. They also enumerate the aspects of deteriorations in human rights, such as impoverishment and lowering standards of living, increasing inequality, scrimination, deprivation of satisfaction of basic needs such as food, clean water, housing, and illiteracy etc. The impact of the adverse consequences of globalization on the enjoyment of human rights is multidimensional; all aspects of human existence be they political, economic, social or cultural, are affected. The negative impact on one dimension of human rights, e.g. economic rights, necessarily has a domino effect on other rights.

The Charter of the United Nations recognizes the important linkages between the maintenance of international peace and security, the establishment of conditions of economic and social progress and development, and the promotion and protection of universal human rights (Charter of the United Nations, 1945). A singularly important development is the imposition by the Charter of a legal obligation on Member States to take joint and separate action in cooperation with the Organization to promote, *inter alia,* higher standards of living, full employment and conditions of economic and social progress and development, and universal respect for, and observance of, human rights (Charter of the United Nations, 1945). Action taken by Member States, either collectively or singly, to defeat this pledge is clearly a violation of the Charter, which under certain circumstances may amount to violations of principles of jus cogens The Copenhagen Declaration and Programme of Action, while recognizing the benefits of globalization, cautions: "At the same time, the rapid processes of change and adjustment have been accompanied by intensified poverty, unemployment and social disintegration. Threats to human well-being, such as environmental risks, have also been globalized. Furthermore, the global transformations of the world economy are profoundly changing the parameters of social development in all countries.

The challenge is how to manage these processes and threats so as to enhance their benefits and mitigate their negative effects upon people" (Report of the World Summit for Social Development, 1995). These very same sentiments are expressed in the Statement of the Committee on Economic, Social and Cultural Rights on globalization issued in May 1998 (International Human Rights Reports, 1999). It calls on the World Bank, the IMF and WTO to devise methods of measuring the impact of their policies on the enjoyment of economic, social and cultural rights (social monitoring) and to revise those policies accordingly (Globalizing Economy Meeting, 2000).

The U.N. General Assembly Resolution "International Convention on the Protection of the Rights of All Migrant Workers and Members of their Families" (1990) contained direct verbiage in regards to the protection of migrant workers and their families from exploitation and servitude, stating that migrants and their families "shall have the freedom of thought, conscience and religion". In 2001, U.N. Secretary General, Kofi Annan, urged universal ratification on International Migrants Day (December 18), noting: ...the fate of many migrants lies in stark contrast to the aspirations reflected in the Universal Declaration of Human Rights, human rights norms and labour conventions (Waldron, 2010). The commitment of the United Nations to the indivisibility of human rights is reflected in the Universal Declaration of Human Rights. This instrument recognizes the right to an adequate standard of living, social security, the right to work and just and favourable conditions of work, and the right to education, in addition to traditional civil and political rights. Significantly, the Universal Declaration of Human Rights also recognizes the right of everyone to a social and international order in which the rights and freedoms set forth in it can be fully realized (Art. 28). Furthermore, the Universal Declaration of Human Rights explicitly recognizes that nothing in it may be interpreted as implying a right to destroy any of the recognized rights. The International Covenants on Economic, Social and Cultural Rights (ICESCR) and on Civil and Political Rights (ICCPR) further elabourate upon the foundation laid by the Universal Declaration of Human Rights. Both have been ratified by large numbers of States and are extremely important in pinpointing the specific legal obligations of State actors with regard to all aspects of human rights protection. The right to development is of equal importance when examining the human rights implications of globalization. The international community through the General Assembly has recognized the right to development as an inalienable human right (Declaration on the Right to Development). The UNDP Human Development Report, 1999 argues that reaping the benefits of a globalized economy cannot be done by merely forcing countries to open up their economies. To make the most of those benefits there has to be a policy package. Governments have to ensure that sound policies for social development and protection, poverty eradication, income distribution and environmental protection are put in place, just as well-thought-out macro-economic policies and institutions have to be established to ensure sound economic management. In the absence of that combination, sustained and sustainable development will remain illusory.

Impact of Globalisation on Human Rights

There are group,of "human rights" in the form of economic rights, labour rights, cultural rights, civil and political rights etc. The globalization is considered to have an impact on the following rights as:

- The admission to the WTO of nations that violate human rights extinguishes opportunities for valuable sanctions to discourage such violations.
- Open trade causes production to relocate to areas where environmental standards are lax and results in environmental degradation. Likewise, the competitive pressures that result from open trade cause regulators to lose control over local regulatory matters and precipitate a race to the bottom over matters such as social welfare standards, environmental standards, and worker protection legislation.
- Open trade exacerbates inequality in the distribution of income. Similarly the negative impact of globalization especially on vulnerable sections of the community

results in the violation of various rights guaranteed by various Covenants in particular on the;

- the enjoyment of fundamental aspects of the right to life;
- freedom from cruel, inhuman or degrading treatment;
- freedom from servitude, the right to equality and non-discrimination;
- the right to an adequate standard of living (including the right to adequate food, clothing and housing);
- the right to maintain a high standard of physical and mental health;
- the right to work accompanied by the right to just and fair conditions of labour;
- freedom of association and assembly and the right to collective bargaining, have been severely impaired.

Developing States are, more often than not, compelled by the dynamics of globalization to take measures that negatively impact on the enjoyment of those rights. Globalization has not caused "developing" countries to catch up with the developed world. Inequality has risen during this present globalization period. The developed world - their intellectuals and policy makers - view globalization as "providing good opportunities for their countries and their people." Globalization can be preserved from two angles. One angle is that globalization is a means of increasing the wealth of nations and promoting international trade. However, globalization is a direct cause for the widening economic gap between "developing" countries and "developed" countries. There is relationship between globalization and equality and non-discrimination in a more concrete fashion. The two concepts are central to the corpus and ethos of human rights instruments and practice. The Universal Declaration and other human rights instruments are unequivocal in their declaration that all persons are equal, and that the right to nondiscrimination is a basic and fundamental human right. Inequality and discrimination unfortunately existed long before globalization was recognized as a distinct phenomenon on the international scene.

Among the distinct groups of society upon whom globalization's impact has been most telling, women clearly stand out. Few observers will deny that the general issue of gender relations globally and the question of women's human rights specifically, has undergone significant transformation. Spurred on by the various international conferences, declarations and most significantly, by the Convention on the Elimination of All Forms of Discrimination against Women, the respect for and recognition of women's human rights has made significant advances worldwide. The phenomenon of globalization adds greater complexities to this quest, particularly in the economic arena, but also within the context of culture and politics. Women in the agricultural sector have also been adversely affected by the promotion of export-oriented economic policies, trade liberalization and TNCs' activities in agriculture related industries. Emphasis on export crops has displaced women workers in certain countries from permanent agricultural employment into seasonal employment. Subsistence farming has been severely affected in the new economic environment, leaving women farmers to seek seasonal employment (United Nations, 1999). Aside from the tenuous and low economic returns of seasonal agricultural employment, the Food and Agriculture Organization of the United Nations (FAO) has noted that the destruction of subsistence farming, increased industrial pollution and the loss of land to large commercial ventures, often financed by TNCs, have given rise to grave problems relating to food security and the health of the rural poor.

It is increasingly becoming clear that it is no longer tenable to draw a neat distinction between the nature of State obligations with regard to civil and political rights on the one hand, and economic, social and cultural rights on the other. United Nations human rights mechanisms have debunked the traditional view that civil and political rights entail only negative obligations, while economic, social and cultural rights give rise to the more complex issue of positive State obligations which require resources to be expended. The United Nations Human Rights Committee has interpreted certain rights guaranteed by the ICCPR as entailing positive obligations. This is clearly the case with regard to the right to life.

The negative effects of corporations on human rights in development can be divided into two categories. First, the corporation may directly violate human rights by itself or in conjunction with another actor. This typically involves civil and political rights, such as the right to personal security. The second category concerns indirect effects. This involves the corporation's influence on host governments. Corporations can undermine the state's ability to fulfill human rights law. They use their influence to encourage governments to adopt policies of liberalization, deregulation and privatization that ignore human rights consequences. This second effect concerns mostly economic, social and cultural rights, which are vital in developing states.

Corporations are the engines of economic growth upon which states depend for the provision of the right to development. Increasingly, corporations are more economically powerful and influential than the developing host-states from which they extract their profits. Members of the World Trade Organization when negotiating and implementing international rules on trade liberalization, should bear in mind their concurrent obligations to promote and protect human rights, mindful of the commitment made in the Vienna Declaration, 1993, that human rights are the first responsibility of governments. While the WTO agreements provide a legal framework for the economic aspects of the liberalization of trade, the norms and standards of human rights balance this by offering a legal framework for trade liberalization's social and ethical dimensions. The human rights violations resulting from globalization are failures of governance. Human rights law is capable of monitoring and regulating foreign investment. Respect for human rights requires governments to protect, promote and fulfill obligations.

The right to development process can provide a framework focused on the implementation of a rights-based approach to development. The right to development is versatile and promotes global responsibility for globalization. The Declaration on the Right to Development requires states to guarantee rights in a manner applicable to globalization. In order to be universal and remain relevant, human rights law must protect those marginalized by the exigencies of globalization by empowering local peoples. Development strategy consists of liberal trading regimes with a reduced role for the state. Despite the new challenges arising from the globalization process and, the state remains the only full subject of international law responsible under human rights law. It is the state, acting individually or collectively, that ultimately controls international relations.

The protection of rights generally requires a legal system that is effective and credible, and such systems do not come free. Moreover, many rights require some additional sacrifice of other human wants—minimum wages, rights to unionize, environmental standards, and social security systems, for example, all come at the price of an increase in the cost of goods and services, or an increase in taxation. Not all effects of globalization will infringe "human rights," but some of them may.

Conclusion

In an age of globalization, the struggle for human rights has become more complex and challenging. Realizing human rights especially economic and social rights is becoming increasingly difficult. One of the most profound challenges that we face as a community of nations is to understand better the emerging socio-economic forces and forms of globalization, to shape them to serve our needs and to respond effectively to their deleterious consequences. Human rights can balance forces of globalisation within a just international legal framework. Maintaining balance between globalisation and protection of human rights should be a priority. Human rights are what make us human. They are the principles by which we create the sacred home for human dignity. Human rights are what reason requires and conscience commands.

REFERENCES

1. Addo, M Human Rights Standards and the Responsibility of Transnational Corporation.
2. Chunakara, M., G. Globalization and Its Impact on Human Rights.
3. McGlodrick, D The Human Rights Committee: Its Role in the Development of the International Covenant on Civil and Political Rights.
4. Oloka-Onyango, J., & Udagama, D The Realization of Economic, Social and Cultural Rights: Globalization and Its Impact on the Full Enjoyment of Human Rights.
5. Rabet, Delphine. Human Rights and Globalization: The Myth of Corporate Social Responsibility? Journal of Alternative Perspectives in the Social Sciences, 1(2), 463-75.
6. Stephens, B. The Amorality of Profit: Transnational Corporations and Human Rights.
7. Waldron S., M. Globalization and Its Impact on the Development and Protection of Human Rights Evaluations and Recommendations.

Human Rights Management after Globalization **Pages 44-52**
Edited by: **Dr. Rabi Narayana Misra**
ISBN: 978-93-88854-05-4
Edition: **2019**
Published by: **Discovery Publishing House Pvt. Ltd., New Delhi (India)**

Chapter 5

Human Rights for Children's in India

[1]Dr. Rabi N. Misra
[2]Dr. K. Ratna Manikyam

Introduction

Although India has a large number of laws to protect and promote the rights of children, children's concerns are viewed primarily as a welfare issue, rather an issue of rights. By developing a legal rights-based approach for children, the Child Rights Initiative combats the violation of children's rights and increases their ability access to the legal system. CRI's, major activity is to do Public Interest Cases in the Supreme Court of India and various High Courts on the issues affecting children. CRI provides pro-bono legal services to children in conflict with the law and children in need of care and protection in the Juvenile Justice Boards and Child Welfare Committees all over the country. CRI represents children who are victim of sexual abuse or victim of bonded labour during the trail proceedings in trial courts, assisting the prosecution in the trial. CRI is a premier agency in the country for providing trainings to police, labour department, civil society organizations, judiciary and government officials on various legislations and policies made for children. CRI has been instrumental in providing assistance in formulation of new laws, rules and policies for children. CRI conducts fact-findings, campaigns, publishes books and poster, organizes consultations, meetings and Judicial Colloquiums for increasing awareness about child rights among duty bearers and right holders

1 Prof. MBA, B.P.U.T. Odisha
2 Government College (A) Rajahmundry, Andhra Pradesh

CRI is part of the Special Taskforce for the rescue and rehabilitation of child labourers and responds to crisis situations through raid and rescue operations. We have set up a Crisis Intervention Center in the Northwest and Central Districts of Delhi, which is also now being replicated in other States. We also monitor the implementation of various schemes and policies related to children. CRI functions in close collabouration with other grassroots organizations in the country.

Issues of Concern

- Child labour
- Child trafficking
- Right to education
- Child health and nutrition
- Child marriages
- Juvenile Justice
- Child sexual abuse
- Torture and Abuse of Children

Major Impacts

Public Interest Cases done by lawyers associated with CRI have brought relief to millions of children in this country. Bachpan Bachao Andolan versus UOI & Ors, though initially brought in Supreme Court for children working in circus industry is set to mark a tremendous impact on child rights in this country as Supreme Court has expanded the scope of this PIL to include each and every aspect of rights of children. In its latest order, Supreme Court has directed all the States to implement the provisions of Juvenile Justice (Care and Protection of Children) Act, 2000 and to constitute Juvenile Justice Boards, Child Welfare Committees, and Special Juvenile Police Units in every district. Avinash Mehrotra vs. Union of India and Ors. was filed when CRI found a lot of children dying due to school building disasters and fire etc. Schools were directed to follow bare minimum safety standards in addition to complying with the National Building Code of India, 2005, with particular emphasis on the Code of Practice for fire safety in Educational Institutions, as enumerated in the Bureau of Indian Standards. In PUCL Vs. Union of India, Court directed State to ensure the right to food and adequate nutrition for children through the Integrated Child Development Programme (ICDS), which benefited approximately 8,30,90,382 children of the country between 0 to six years of age. The Supreme Court also directed the State Governments/Union Territories to implement the Mid Day Meal Scheme, ensuring mid day meals to approximately 100 million children across the country. The mid-day meal has been shown to contribute significantly to the lowering of levels of malnutrition among children. Forum for Fact Finding and Documentation Vs. Union of India, directions were issued that each state in India notifies the rules for the Prohibition of Child Marriages Act, 2006. Another Supreme Court case Sampurna Behura Vs. Union of India significantly changed the scenarios *vis a vis* implementation of the Juvenile Justice Act, as a result of which Juvenile Justice Boards and child Welfare Committees have been constituted in each district of every state in India. CRI has done a number of public interest cases (See Reena Banerjee Vs. Govt. of Delhi) in several states for improving the way child care institutions are being run, significantly improving the quality of care to children in such institutions.

The CRI has saved hundreds of children by conducting rescue interventions in over 170 cases of children being exploited as domestic workers, stopping over 200 child marriages, and facilitating the arrest and prosecution of child traffickers. The CRI has set up a model for legal aid for Juveniles in Delhi, which is being replicated now all over the country gradually. CRI's lawyers have consistently struggled to eliminate anti-child practices from functioning of police by initiating legal action in a number of cases where children are illegal detained or tortured at police stations. On the other hand CRI's trainings to police, members of juvenile justice boards, child welfare committees and government authorities have brought a sea-impact on the quality of service delivery to children.

Child Rights Initiative

Although India has a large number of laws to protect and promote the rights of children, children's concerns are viewed primarily as a welfare issue, rather an issue of rights. By developing a legal rights-based approach for children, the Child Rights Initiative combats the violation of children's rights and increases their ability access to the legal system.

Teacher Convicted for Raping a Minor Student

In February 2016, the Hon'ble Sessions Court in Srinagar announced the conviction of "13 Years" imprisonment to a teacher who had raped a minor girl. The case was filed in 2013 against the teacher who raped her 14 year old student.

SC direct States to clear pendency in Juvenile Justice Boards in Sampurna Behrua Case.

SC direct States to clear pendency in Juvenile Justice Boards - Another HRLN achievement towards ensuring child rights.

Highlights of the Judgement in W.P. (Civil) 473/2005.

- "It is mandated that every State should have a Juvenile Justice Board in place in every District on or before 31st December, 2015."
- "It is made clear that there is no prohibition in law in having more than one Juvenile Justice Board in a District depending upon the number of pending inquiries and the distance involved in moving children from the Observation Home to the venue of the Juvenile Justice Board. Therefore, it is made clear that a District can have more than one Juvenile Justice Board."
- "As regards vacancies, we direct that all vacancies in the Juvenile Justice Boards should be filled up on or before 31st December, 2015 in accordance with Rule 92 of the Juvenile Justice (Care and Protection of Children) Rules, 2007 (for short "the Rules") by a Selection Committee presided over by a retired Judge of the High Court."

A ghastly incident of gang rape took place in a moving bus in the streets of Delhi. In connection with the said incident six accused were arrested on 22.12.2012, one of whom, namely, the first respondent in the present special leave petition was a juvenile on the date of the occurrence of the crime. The victim of the offence died on 29.1.2013. While the Juvenile Justice Board (hereinafter for short "the Board") was in session of the matter against the first respondent, the petitioners in the special leave petition approached the Board seeking implement in the proceedings before the Board and an interpretation of the provisions of the Juvenile Justice (Care and Protection of Children) Act, 2000 (hereinafter for short 'the JJ Act') so as to enable the prosecution of the first respondent in a regular criminal court.

The Hon. Supreme Court by dismissing the petition upheld the constitutional validity of the J.J. Act, 2000 (2006) and stated that "If the provisions of the Act clearly indicate the legislative intent in the light of the country's international commitments and the same is in conformity with the constitutional requirements, it is not necessary for the Court to understand the legislation in any other manner. In fact, if the Act is plainly read and understood, which we must do, the resultant effect thereof is wholly consistent with the Act, therefore, need not be read down, as suggested, to save it from the vice of unconstitutionality for article 14 are such unconstitutionality does not exist"

Child marriage has been an issue in India for a long time. Because of its root in traditional, cultural and religious practises it has been a hard battle to fight. Child marriage is also associated with other problems like dowry and child widowhood. It is also associated with malnutrition, poor health of mothers and high fertility and hence over-population. Thus, it is imperative to have a legislation in place to fix the above mentioned issues. Therefore, The Prohibition of Child Marriage Act was enacted in 2006. The following is an overview of the act.

According to the act a child is a male who has not completed twenty one years of age and a female who has not completed eighteen years of age. Child marriage is a contract between any two people of which either one or both parties is a child. This is the major reason why a child is not permitted to enter into marriage.

Even though marriage generally comes in the purview of personal laws, this Act is an overall legislation which clearly states that marriage of a child (as explained above) is not permitted under any circumstances.

Summary on United Nations Convention on the Rights of the Child

India ratified the United Nations Convention on the Rights of the Child (henceforth referred as UNCRC) in the Parliament on llth December, 1992. The key ingredients of the UNCRC are as follows:

(*a*) The UNCRC defines the child as a person under 18 years of age. It acknowledges the primary role of parents and the family in the care and protection of children, as well as the obligation of the State to help them carry out these duties.

(*b*) The UN Convention consists of 41 articles, each of which details a different type of right. These rights are not ranked in order of importance; instead they interact with one another to form one integrated set of rights. A common approach is to group these articles together under the following themes:

- Survival rights: include the child's right to life and the needs that are most basic to existence, such as nutrition, shelter, an adequate living standard, and access to medical services.
- Development rights: include the right to education, play, leisure, cultural activities, access to information, and freedom of thought, conscience and religion.
- Protection rights: ensure children are safeguarded against all forms of abuse, neglect and exploitation, including special care for refugee children; safeguards for children in the criminal justice system; protection for children in employment; protection and rehabilitation for children who have suffered exploitation or abuse of any kind.
- Participation rights: encompass children's freedom to express opinions, to have a say in matters affecting their own lives, to join associations and to assemble peacefully. As their capacities develop, children should have increasing opportunity to participate in the activities of society, in preparation for adulthood.

(*c*) The UN Convention includes four articles that are given special emphasis. These are also known as 'general principles'. These rights are the bedrock for securing the additional rights in the UN Convention:

1. That all the rights guaranteed by the UNCRC must be available to all children without discrimination of any kind (Article 2);
2. That the best interests of the child must be a primary consideration in all actions concerning children (Article 3);
3. That every child has the right to life, survival and development (Article 6); and
4. That the child's view must be considered and taken into account in all matters affecting him or her (Article 12).

The Protection of Children from Sexual Offences Act, 2012

The Protection of Children from Sexual Offences Act, 2012 seeks to protect children from offences such as sexual assault, sexual harassment and pornography. India is a signatory to the UN Convention on the Rights of the Child since 1992. The parties to the Convention are required to take measures to prevent children from being coerced into any unlawful sexual activity. Any person below the age of 18 years is defined as a "child". The Act seeks to penalise any person who commits offences such as "sexual harassment", "sexual assault", "penetrative sexual assault", and "aggravated penetrative sexual assault"

A person shall be guilty of using a child for pornographic purposes if he uses a child in any form of media for the purpose of sexual gratification through representation of sexual organs of a child or using a child in sexual acts or other types of obscene representation. The penalty is rigorous imprisonment for up to five years and a fine. On subsequent convictions, the term of imprisonment is up to 7 years and fine.

The Major Aspects to Right to Education Act include

The Constitution (Eighty-sixth Amendment) Act, 2002 inserted Article 21-A in the Constitution of India to provide free and compulsory education of all children in the age group of six to fourteen years as a Fundamental Right in such a manner as the State may, by law, determine. The Right of Children to Free and Compulsory Education (RTE) Act, 2009, which represents the consequential legislation envisaged under Article 21-A, means that every child has a right to full time elementary education of satisfactory and equitable quality in a formal school which satisfies certain essential norms and standards.

Article 21-A & the RTE Act came into effect on 1 April, 2010. The title of the RTE Act incorporates the words 'free and compulsory'. 'Free education' means that no child, other than a child who has been admitted by his or her parents to a school which is not supported by the appropriate Government, shall be liable to pay any kind of fee or charges or expenses which may prevent him or her from pursuing and completing elementary education. 'Compulsory education' casts an obligation on the appropriate Government and local authorities to provide and ensure admission, attendance and completion of elementary education by all children in the 6-14 age group. With this, India has moved forward to a rights based framework that casts a legal obligation on the Central and State Governments to implement this fundamental child right as enshrined in the Article 21-A of the Constitution, in accordance with the provisions of the RTE Act.

The Juvenile Justice (Care and Protection of Children) Act, 2000 is an Act to fulfil its commitment to the United Nations Convention on the Rights of the Child which is ratified on 11th December, 1992. In this act a child or juvenile is defined as a person who has not completed his/her 18th year of age. This is an act consolidate and amend the law relating to juvenjles in conflict with law and children in need of care and protection, by providing for proper care, protection and treatment by catering to their development needs, and by adopting a child-friendly approach in the adjudication and disposition of matters in the best interest of children and for their ultimate rehabilitation through various institutions established under this enactment.

The Constitution has, in several provisions, including clause (3) of article 15, clauses (e) and (f) of article 39, articles

45 and 47, imposes on the State a primary responsibility of ensuring that all the needs of children are met and that their basic human rights are fully protected. The Act is one of the key instruments in legislation for the protection of children. The most striking feature of the Act is that it distinguishes between a child and an adult in terms of trial and conviction of offenses.

This Act ensures that offenses committed by children are being analysed. Thus a child who commits an offense will not be treated in the same light as an adult. The nature of the offense, circumstances and atmosphere in which the child committed the act and such other factors are analysed before convicting the juvenile. The juvenile is usually tried in a special Children's Court.

Canclusion

The Act was amended in 2006 to strengthen the provisions for children. It makes the Act much more effective. The amendments made to the Act have led to large scale deliberations and decisions which have been made for the benefit of the children.

The Situation of Children in India- A Profile.

The following report contains a detailed analysis of the situation of children in India. Prepared by the UNICEF. This report deals with various issues like child health, education, maternal health, child mortality, disparities between children, and the like. It has a far reaching analysis containing information on many topics related to the child, what fosters or restricts his development and so on.

This report becomes essential as it is an indicator to the real scenario of children in India. The report contains statistics of the various problems faced by a child. These analysis cover majority of the nation and also provide for regulations and measures to combat the same.

This report is essential for research and development with respect to the situation of children in India. It helps in curbing the problem by highlighting the blunt reality existing in our country.

Human Rights Management after Globalization **Pages 53-65**
Edited by: **Dr. Rabi Narayana Misra**
ISBN: 978-93-88854-05-4
Edition: **2019**
Published by: **Discovery Publishing House Pvt. Ltd., New Delhi (India)**

Chapter 6

Human Rights and the Indian Constitution

[1]Smt. Bandita Panda
[2]P.L. Naidu

Introduction

Human Rights are generally defined as the rights which every human being is entitled to enjoy and to have protected. Human rights are commonly understood as "inalienable fundamental rights to which a person is inherently entitled simply because she or he is a human being." Human Right mean the rights relating to life, liberty, equality and dignity of the individual grananteed under the Constitution or embodied in the International Covenants and enforceable by courts.

Human rights are thus conceived as universal (applicable everywhere) and egalitarian (the same for everyone). These rights may exist as natural rights or as legal rights, in both national and international law. The struggle for the recognition of human rights and the struggle against political, economic, social and cultural oppression, against injustice and inequalities, have been an integral part of the history of all human societies.

Historical Background

The origins of the contemporary conception of human rights can be traced to the period of the Renaissance and later of the Enlightenment of which humanism may be said to be the heart and soul. The issue of fundamental or (also called) human right became an issue of prominence and fundamental significance since the last two hundred years only.

---

1 Dept. of MA, MBA, H.R. Manager, New Delhi.
2 Economics Government Degree College Kothapeta, Andhra Pradesh.

First of all Magna Carta (Charter of Liberty) was promulgated on June 15, 1215.

In 1225 King Andrew II of Hungary issued the Golden Bill in the words of Magna Carta.

In 1283 King Peter III of Aragon bestowed upon his subjects the Law of Privileges.

In 1355 British Parliament re-affirmed the declaration of Magna Carta and introduced the words due process of law. It stated, No man of what state or condition so ever he be, shall be put out of his lands or tenements nor taken nor imprisoned nor put to death, without he be brought in to answer by due process of law. In 1689 the British Parliament passed the Bill of Rights which Lord Acton described as the greatest thing done by the English nation.

In 1690 John Locke propagated theory of social contract attempting to reconcile sovereignty and democracy.

There were two great revolutions at the end of 18th century, in America and in France inspired by philosophers like Samuel Adams, Jefferson, Rousseau and Kant who emphasized on the Law of Nature and the natural rights of man. Similarly in Virginia in 1776, Declaration of Rights was promulgated which guaranteed freedom of press and religion, rights to jury trial and other safeguards of a criminal trial. It made the military authorities to civil power and provided for free elections. In 1776 there was also the declaration of American independence drafted by John Locke. The preamble read: All men are created equal that they are endowed by their Creator with certain inalienable rights that among these are life, liberty and the pursuit of happiness.

In 1789 the American Congress passed the Bill of Rights in the shape often amendments of the Constitution. While in France the French Assembly adopted the Declaration of the Rights of Man and the Citizen. It recited: Men are born free and equal in rights, aim of every political association is the preservation of the practical and imperceptible right of man. The rights are liberty, property, security and resistance to oppression.

The fourth Amendment of the American constitution in 1868 stipulated: No state shall deprive any person of life, liberty or property without due process of law, nor deny to any person within its jurisdiction, the equal protection of law.

In the 18th and 19th centuries the basic human rights were included in the constitutions of various nations, Sweden, Spain, Norway, Belgium, Sardinia, Denmark and Switzerland, Russia, Turkey, China, etc.

In 1917 the Declaration of the Rights of the working and Exploited People was issued by the All-Russian Congress of Soviets.

In 1930 on January, 26th people of all over India taken the Pledge of Independence at thousands of meeting held all over the country.

In 1931 March, the Indian National Congress in its session at Karachi adopted the resolution of Fundamental Rights and Economic Programme.

In 1941 President Roosevelt stressed on four freedoms, Freedom of speech, Freedom of Religion, Freedom from Want and Freedom from Fear.

The same year Winston Churchill wanted to ensure that the war ended, with the enthronement of human rights.

France in the preamble of its Constitution of 1946 reaffirmed: Every human being without distinction of race, religion or belief possesses inalienable and sacred rights.

The 1946 Constitution of Japan provided: The people shall not be prevented from enjoying any of the fundamental rights.

On 22nd January, 1947, the Constituent Assembly of India adopted the resolution of India' Charter of Freedom.

During the last decades the emphasis on fundamental rights reached its climax with the formation of the UNO after the Second World War and the subsequent drafting of the Universal Declaration of Human Rights.

The United Nations Charter which came in to effect on 24th October, 1945, reflected the aspirations of the peoples who affirmed faith in 'fundamental human rights' and 'in the dignity and worth of the human person'.

The Universal Declaration of Human Rights (UDHR) is a milestone document in the history of human rights. Drafted by representatives with different legal and cultural backgrounds from all regions of the world, the Declaration was proclaimed by the United Nations General Assembly in Paris on 10 December, 1948 General Assembly resolution 217 A (111) (French) (Spanish) as a common standard of achievements for all peoples and all nations. It sets out, for the first time, fundamental human rights to be universally protected.

International Treaties

In 1966, the International Covenant on Civil and Political Rights (ICCPR) and the International Covenant on Economic, Social and Cultural Rights (ICESCR) were adopted by the United Nations, between them making the rights contained in the UDHR binding on all states that have signed this treaty, creating human-rights law.

Since then numerous other treaties (pieces of legislation) have been offered at the international level. They are generally known as human rights instruments. Some of the most significant, referred to (with ICCPR and ICESCR) as "the seven core treaties", are:

Convention on the Elimination of All Forms of Racial Discrimination (CERD) (adopted 1966, entry into force: 1969).

Convention on the Elimination of All Forms of Discrimination against Women (CEDAW) (adopted 1979, entry into force: 1981):

- United Nations Convention against Torture (CAT) (adopted 1984, entry into force: 1984).
- United Nations Declaration on the Right to Development adopted 1986.
- Convention on the Rights of the Child (CRC) (adopted 1989, entry into force: 1989).
- The Vienna Declaration and Programme of Action, 1993 (Endorsed by the General Assembly of the United Nations).

- International Convention on the Protection of the Rights of All Migrant Workers and Members of their Families (ICRMW or more often MWC) (adopted 1990, entry into force: 2003).
- Convention on the Rights of Persons with Disabilities (CRPD) (adopted 2006, entry into force: 2008).

Human Rights Enshrined in Indian Constitution

Human Rights in Indian Constitution can be found in the Preamble of the Constitution of India, Part III of the Constitution on Fundamental Rights and Part IV of the Constitution on Directive Principles, which together have been described as forming the core of the Constitution which together reflect the basic principles of the Universal Declaration of Human Rights and the Covenants on Civil and Political Rights, Economic, Social and Cultural Rights, and Part IV-A of the Constitution on Fundamental Duties, Articles 300A, 325 and 326.

Preamble

The Preamble to the Constitution of India is a brief introductory statement that sets out the guiding purpose and principles of the document.

That the preamble is not an integral part of the Indian constitution was first decided upon by the Supreme Court of India in the Beru Bari case, therefore it is not enforceable in a court of law. However, the Supreme Court of India has, in the Kesavananda case, recognized that the preamble may be used to interpret ambiguous areas of the constitution where differing interpretations present themselves. In the 1995 case of Union Government Vs. LIC of India also the Supreme Court has once again held that the Preamble is an integral part of the Constitution.

As originally enacted the preamble described the state as a "sovereign democratic republic". In 1976 the Forty-second Amendment changed this to read "sovereign socialist secular democratic republic".

PREAMBLE FULL TEXT

Preamble

WE, THE PEOPLE OF INDIA, having solemnly resolved to constitute India into a

SOVEREIGN SOCIALIST SECULAR DEMOCRATIC REPUBLIC and to secure to all its citizens:

JUSTICE, social, economic and political;

LIBERTY of thought, expression, belief, faith and worship;

EQUALITY of status and of opportunity;

and to promote among them all

FRATERNITY assuring the dignity of the individual and the unity and integrity of the Nation;

IN OUR CONSTITUENT ASSEMBLY this twenty-sixth day of November, 1949, do HEREBY ADOPT, ENACT AND GIVE TO OURSELVES THIS CONSTITUTION.

The Fundamental Rights

The Fundamental rights are defined as basic human freedoms which every Indian citizen has the right to enjoy for a proper and harmonious development of personality.

These rights universally apply to all citizens, irrespective of race, place of birth, religion, caste, creed, colour or Gender. They are enforceable by the courts, subject to certain restrictions.

The six fundamental rights recognized by the constitution are:

Right to Equality

Right to equality is an important right provided for in Articles 14, 15, 16, 17 and 18 of the constitution. It is the principal foundation of all other rights and liberties, and guarantees the following:

Equality before law: Article 14 of the constitution guarantees that all citizens shall be equally protected by the laws of the country. It means that the State cannot discriminate any of the Indian citizens on the basis of their caste, creed, colour, sex, gender, religion or place of birth.

Social equality and equal access to public areas: Article 15 of the constitution states that no person shall be discriminated on the basis of caste, colour, language etc. Every person shall have equal access to public places like public parks, museums, wells, bathing ghats and temples etc.

Equality in matters of public employment: Article 16 of the constitution lays down that the State cannot discriminate against anyone in the matters of employment. All citizens can apply for government jobs. There are some exceptions.

Abolition of untouchability: Article 17 of the constitution abolishes the practice of untouchability. Practice of untouchability is an offense and anyone doing so is punishable by law.

Abolition of Titles: Article 18 of the constitution prohibits the State from conferring any titles. Citizens of India cannot accept titles from a foreign State. However, Military and academic distinctions can be conferred on the citizens of India. The awards of Bharat Ratna and Padma Vibhushan cannot be used by the recipient as a title.

Right to Freedom

The Constitution of India contains the right to freedom, given in articles 19, 20, 21 and 22, with the view of guaranteeing individual rights that were considered vital by the framers of the constitution.

The right to freedom in Article 19 guarantees the following six freedoms:

Freedom of speech and expression, which enable an individual to participate in public activities. Reasonable restrictions can be imposed in the interest of public order, security of State, decency or morality.

Freedom to assemble peacefully without arms, on which the State can impose reasonable restrictions in the interest of public order and the sovereignty and integrity of India.

Freedom to form associations or unions on which the State can impose reasonable restrictions on this freedom in the interest of public order, morality and the sovereignty and integrity of India.

Freedom to move freely throughout the territory of India though reasonable restrictions can be imposed on this right in the interest of the general public.

Freedom to reside and settle in any part of the territory of India which is also subject to reasonable restrictions by the State in the interest of the general public or for the protection of the scheduled tribes.

Freedom to practice any profession or to carry on any occupation, trade or business on which the State may impose reasonable restrictions in the interest of the general public.

The constitution guarantees the right to life and personal liberty, which in turn cites specific provisions in which these rights are applied and enforced:

Protection with respect to conviction for offences is guaranteed in the right to life and personal liberty.

According to **Article 20,**

- No one can be awarded punishment which is more than what the law of the land prescribes at that time.
- Moreover, no person accused of any offence shall be compelled to be a witness against himself.
- The other principle enshrined in this article is no person can be convicted twice for the same offence.
- Protection of life and personal liberty is also stated under right to life and personal liberty.

Article 21 Declares that no citizen can be denied his life and liberty except by law.

Article 21(A) Makes a fundamental right of every child to get free and compulsory education. Rights of a person arrested under ordinary circumstances are laid down in the right to life and personal liberty.

Article 22 No one can be arrested without being told the grounds for his arrest.

Also an arrested citizen has to be brought before the nearest magistrate within 24 hours.

The constitution also imposes restrictions on these rights. The government restricts these freedoms in the interest of the independence, sovereignty and integrity of India. In the interest of morality and public order, the government can also impose restrictions. However, the right to life and personal liberty cannot be suspended. The six freedoms are also automatically suspended or have restrictions imposed on them during a state of emergency.

Right Against Exploitation

Child labour and Begar is prohibited under Right against exploitation.

The right against exploitation, given in Articles 23 and 24, provides for two provisions.

Article 23: The abolition of trafficking in human beings and *Begar* (forced labour).

Article 24: Abolition of employment of children below the age of 14 years in dangerous jobs like factories and mines.

An exception is made in employment without payment for compulsory services for public purposes. Compulsory military conscription is covered by this provision.

Right to Freedom of Religion

Right to freedom of religion, covered in Articles 25, 26, 27 and 28,

Article 23: Provides religious freedom to all citizens of India.

Article 24: Religious communities can set up charitable institutions of their own.

Article 25: No person shall be compelled to pay taxes for the promotion of a particular religion.

Article 26: State run institution cannot impart education that is pro-religion.

Cultural and Educational Rights

Articles 29 and **30** are there to protect the rights of the minorities.

Article 29: Any community which has a language and a script of its own has the right to conserve and develop it. No citizen can be discriminated against for admission in State or State aided institutions.

Article 30: All minorities, religious or linguistic, can set up their own educational institutions to preserve and develop their own culture. In granting aid to institutions, the State cannot discriminate against any institution on the basis of the fact that it is administered by a minority institution.

RIGHT TO LIFE

In recent judgment Supreme Court of India extended scope of right to life which was mentioned earlier.

Right to Constitutional Remedies

This right covered under Article 32 of the Constitution.

Article 32 empowers the citizens to move a court of law in case of any denial of the fundamental rights.

This procedure of asking the courts to preserve or safeguard the citizens' fundamental rights can be done in various ways. The courts can issue various kinds of writs. These writs are habeas corpus, mandamus, prohibition, quo warrant and certiorari. When a national or state emergency is declared, this right is suspended by the Central Government.

RIGHT TO PROPERTY WAS ORIGINALLY A FUNDAMENTAL RIGHT, BUT IS NOW A LEGAL RIGHT

Directive Principles of State Policy

The Directive Principles of State Policy, embodied in Part IV of the Constitution, are directions given to the State to guide the establishment of an economic and social democracy, as proposed by the Preamble. The State is expected to keep these principles in mind while framing laws and policies, even though they are non-justifiable in nature. The Directive Principles may be classified under the following categories: ideals that the State ought to strive towards achieving; directions for the exercise of legislative and executive power; and rights of the citizens which the State must aim towards securing.

Article 37, while stating that the Directive Principles are not enforceable in any court of law, declares them to be "fundamental to the governance of the country" and imposes an obligation on the State to apply them in matters of legislation.

Article 38 emphasize the positive duty of the State to promote the welfare of the people by affirming social, economic and political justice, as well as to fightincome inequality and ensure individual dignity, in order to ensure equitable distribution of land resources.

Article 39 lays down certain principles of policy to be followed by the State, including providing an adequate means of livelihood for all citizens, equal pay for equal work for men and women, proper working conditions, reduction of the concentration of wealth and means of production from the hands of a few, and distribution of community resources to "sub serve the common good".

Article 39A requires the State to provide free legal aid to ensure that opportunities for securing justice are available to all citizens irrespective of economic or other disabilities. Article 40 states The State shall also work for organization of village panchayats and help enable them to function as units of self-government.

Article 41 states The State shall Endeavour to provide the right to work, to education and to public assistance in cases of unemployment, old age, sickness and disablement, within the limits of economic capacity.

Article 42 provide for just and humane conditions of work and maternity relief.

Article 43 The State should also ensure living wage and proper working conditions for workers, with full enjoyment of leisure and social and cultural activities. Also, the promotion of cottage industries in rural areas is one of the obligations of the State.

Article 43A The State shall take steps to promote their participation in management of industrial undertakings.

Article 44 The State shall endeavor to secure a uniform civil code for all citizens.

Article 45 provides free and compulsory education to all children till they attain the age of 14 years. This directive regarding education of children was added by the 86th Amendment Act, 2002.

Article 46 states State should and work for the economic and educational upliftment of castes, scheduled and other weaker sections of the society.

Article 47 commit the State to raise the level of nutrition and the standard of living and to improve public health, particularly by prohibiting intoxicating drinks and drugs injurious to health except for medicinal purposes.

Article 48 State should organize agriculture and animal husbandry on modern and scientific lines by improving breeds and prohibiting slaughter of cows, calves, other mulch and draught cattle.

Article 48A State should protect and improve the environment and safeguard the forests and wildlife of the country. This directive, regarding protection of forests and wildlife was added by the 42nd Amendment Act, 1976.

Article 49 it shall be the obligation of the State to protect the monuments, places and objects of historic and artistic interest and national importance against destruction and damage.

Article 50 states for the separation of judiciary from executive in public services

Article 51 ensure that the State shall strive for the promotion and maintenance of international peace and security, just and honorable relations between nations, respect for international law and treaty obligations, as well as settlement of international disputes by arbitration.

Fundamental Duties

The Fundamental Duties are a novel feature of the Indian Constitution in recent times. Originally, the Constitution of India did not contain these duties. The Forty Second Constitution Amendment Act, 1976 has incorporated ten Fundamental Duties in Article 51 (A) of the Constitution of India. The Eighty-Six Constitution Amendment Act, 2002 has added one more Fundamental Duty in Article 51 (A) of the Constitution of India. As a result, there are now 11 Fundamental Duties of the Citizen of India.

Human Rights Management after Globalization **Pages 66-75**
Edited by: Dr. Rabi Narayana Misra
ISBN: 978-93-88854-05-4
Edition: 2019
Published by: Discovery Publishing House Pvt. Ltd., New Delhi (India)

Chapter 7 Human Rights for Women in India

[1]Dr. S. Badtiya
[2]V.V. Satya

Introduction

Woman, the *very* creation of God that makes living beautiful is often at the receiving end of trauma. Not necessarily do criminals live around rural thatched roofs only. They are found in sky rises and posh suites too. In 2009 rape cases have reached 2,497, domestic violence has crossed the 10,000 mark. In short women are still treated as a lesser person. But of course the government is doing all its best to improvise the situation. Around 2.8 million social workers have been employed by the government to reach into villages and homes across the country, to make women aware of their rights.

Much to their surprise women are not even aware that they have any rights in a man's world. While some are treated as slaves in their adulthood, most don't even enjoy a childhood. To this purpose the relational Commission for Women is set up and located at 4, Deen Dayal, Upadhayaya Marg, New Delhi 110 002, phone: 11 23237166. It is the apex organisation for protecting women. Besides this there are Commissions set up in each state of the country to protect and uplift women.

These organizations implicit that there should be equality of rights for women as given to men. Article 14 of the Constitution in India says that no person will be denied equality before the law. Article 42 states that women should be provided just and

[1] Host Prof. Department of MBA, B.P.U.T. Odisha.
[2] Department of Commerce Government Degree College Ravulapalem, Andhra Pradesh

human work atmosphere and maternity relief. Sati laws have been abolished, child marriages are legally punishable. The girl now has to be of 18 years when she is married and her consent has to be taken. Using force is punishable. To her relief eve teasing too is considered a crime. It can be reported and offenders will be put behind bars immediately.

Women's Rights Movement in India : There are many committed organizations and non-governmental organisations (NGOs) in India working for the advancement of women's rights in addition to government appointed agencies. The Indian government has a National Commission for Women, which is dedicated to the welfare of Indian women.

The violation of women's fundamental rights through physical, mental, emotional, and sexual violence against women has become almost commonplace in the Indian context. Violence against women has taken particularly acute forms in circumstances where populations are already marginalized, such as in areas affected by armed conflict, areas undergoing mass displacement. Women in the Tribal belts and amongst Dalit populations are already vulnerable, and become even more so in areas affected by conflict. There is therefore a pressing need for the judiciary to recognize and address the particular forms of violence levied against women who are 'doubly marginalised' by caste, class, religion, or in situations conflict. Customary routinely laws discriminate against women, both by denying justice to victims of violence and by dispossessing women from their shares in land and property. A number of laws that protect women from discrimination have also either inadequate, or have not been properly implemented. HRLN has been intimately connected with the women's movement for over two decades. The Women's Justice Initiative (WJI) is our national network of lawyers and social activists, using the law to oppose all forms of gender-based discrimination and violence against women and to increase women's access to the justice system as a vital means to their empowerment.

What We Do?

The framework of 'women's justice' involves not only the prevention of specific forms of violence and discrimination against women, but also encompasses all other human rights, including the right to food and health; disability, housing labour rights; dalit/ tribal / adivasi rights; environmental justice; criminal justice, etc. With this holistic vision of equality and gender justice, WJI works directly with poor and marginalized women as well as through legal education, advocacy and policy analysis to continue the struggle for women's rights.

In order to achieve our objectives, the WJI adopts a multi-pronged strategy to deal with the various facets of women's rights violations. The WJI engages in strategic litigation through PILs in the High Courts and the Supreme Court for systematic changes as well as the implementation of policy and women's rights laws. Through legal aid and counseling we provide women with representation women in cases including divorce, domestic violence, matrimonial remedies, guardianship, custody, adoption, property rights, sexual harassment, etc. The WJI is also active in opposing bail of the accused in cases of violence against women, particularly in cases of rape, dowry harassment, domestic violence, and acid-attacks. Lawyers working with the WJI provide legal counseling to women at various women's crime cells, and to women prisoners. We provide legal expertise as member of several committees, including as members of several sexual harassment complaint committees across the country. The WJI also runs a number of helplines throughout the country that provide legal counseling as well as some and psychosocial support to women.

WJI responds to situations of crisis through emergency dispatch of legal teams for support in crisis-affected zones, through investigative missions and through legal fact-findings, which often become the basis for further litigation to address severe women's rights violations. We also consistently monitor and review the implementation of laws and policies related to women.

Through legal education and training for social activists, mahila panchayats, police personnel, lawyers, law students, paralegals, etc., we work to integrate women's issues into the general discourse on justice and human rights. Judicial colloquia and legal consultations is a crucial aspect of our work, to sensitize judges and strategize the development of women's rights law in India. The WJI also supports campaigns to influence public opinion, policies and legislation in support of a violence-free society for women. A core operational element of the WJI is the degree to which the team works in solidarity with other organizations. As such, WJI has nurtured deep partnerships with grassroots women's NGOs, supporting them in the collective struggle to address the public denial of women's rights.

Issues of Concern

- Rape and sexual assault.
- Domestic violence.
- Sexual harassment in the workplace and in educational institutions.
- Matrimonial disputes, custody, divorce.
- Women's property and inheritance rights.
- Reproductive and sexual health rights of women/ adolescent girls.
- Pre-birth sex-selection and elimination of female foetuses.
- Trafficking for commercial sexual exploitation, domestic work, marriage, etc.
- Child marriage.
- Child Sexual Abuse.
- Witch hunting.
- Acid attacks.
- 'Honour' based crimes against women/ 'honour killings'.
- Equal employment opportunities for women and labour rights.
- Rights of doubly marginalized sections of women like HIV+ women, dalit and tribal women, women prisoners, lesbians, bisexuals, disabled women.
- Any other gender based discrimination/exploitation.

Major Impacts

The WJI is combating the various facets of violence against women through the legal system. In a precedent-setting verdict on a case of an acid-attack, brought by WJI lawyers to the Karnataka High Court, the court created legal history by treating the throwing of acid as an-attempt to murder (rather than an attempt to cause grievous injury) and imposed a life sentence on the perpetrator, ensuring that cases of acid-throwing attract stricter punishment, without bail. In a remarkable judgment, Somaru Patel Vs. State, for the first time in judicial history, the court awarded a life sentence under Section 6 of the Immoral Traffic (Prevention) Act, 1956 for the forceful detention of women for prostitution. In another historic case filed in the Delhi High Court, Shramjivi Mahila Samittee Vs. State and Others, the court directed the petitioner to form guidelines for placement agencies for domestic workers, which were drafted by the WJI and submitted to the court for implementation.

HRLN is at the forefront on litigation on women's issues across the country, playing a pivotal role in implementing the guidelines given by the Supreme Court on sexual harassment. The case of Shivani Thakur Vs. State of Punjab, filed by HRLN's unit in Chandigarh, received an order that resulted in the State of Punjab instituting sexual harassment grievance committees in all its departments. HRLN's landmark PIL in the Supreme Court, in the case of Medha Kotwal Lele Vs. Union of India received orders mandating only a single enquiry in cases of sexual harassment to carb the victimization of the complainant. The WJI has also made history by bringing reproductive rights into the ambit of legally enforceable rights through a number of landmark cases and PILs.

The WJI is particularly active in circumstances of extreme violation of women and has used the legal system to ensure rights and provide substantive reliefs in such cases. For example, in a writ petition filed in West Bengal against a shelter home where a woman was refused entry due to her HIV positive status, XY Vs. Union of India, the court directed the directorate of Social Welfare to clarify what steps have been taken to establish more shelter homes for positive woman.

Women Rights in India: Constitutional Rights and Legal Rights

The rights available to woman (ladies) in India can be classified into two categories, namely as constitutional rights and legal rights. The constitutional rights are those which are provided in the various provisions of the constitution. The legal rights, on the other hand, are those which are provided in the various laws (acts) of the Parliament and the State Legislatures.

Constitutional Rights to Women

The rights and safeguards enshrined in the constitution for women in India are listed below:

1. The state shall not discriminate against any citizen of India on the ground of sex **[Article 15(1)].**
2. The state is empowered to make any special provision for women. In other words, this provision enables the state to make affirmative discrimination in favour of women **[Article 15(3)].**
3. No citizen shall be discriminated against or be ineligible for any employment or office under the state on the ground of sex **[Article 16(2)].**
4. Traffic in human beings and forced labour are prohibited **[Article 23(1)].**
5. The state to secure for men and women equally the right to an adequate means of livelihood **[Article 39(a)].**
6. The state to secure equal pay for equal work for both Indian men and women **[Article 39(d)].**
7. The state is required to ensure that the health and strength of women workers are not abused and that they are not forced by economic necessity to enter avocations unsuited to their strength **[Article 39(e)].**
8. The state shall make provision for securing just and humane conditions of work and maternity relief **[Article 42].**

9. It shall be the duty of every citizen of India to renounce practices derogatory to the dignity of women **[Article 51-A(e)].**
10. One-third of the total number of seats to be filled by direct election in every Panchayat shall be reserved for women **[Article 243-D(3)].**
11. One-third of the total number of offices of chairpersons in the Panchayats at each level shall be reserved for women **[Article 243-D(4)].**
12. One-third of the total number of seats to be filled by direct election in every Municipality shall be reserved for women **[Article 243-T(3)].**
13. The offices of chairpersons in the Municipalities shall be reserved for women in such manner as the State Legislature may provide **[Article 243-T(4)].**

Legal Rights to Women

The following various legislation's contain several rights and safeguards for women:

1. Protection of Women from Domestic Violence Act (2005) is a comprehensive legislation to protect women in India from all forms of domestic violence. It also covers women who have been/are in a relationship with the abuser and are subjected to violence of any kind—physical, sexual, mental, verbal or emotional.
2. Immoral Traffic (Prevention) Act (1956) is the premier legislation for prevention of trafficking for commercial sexual exploitation. In other words, it prevents trafficking in women and girls for the purpose of prostitution as an organised means of living.
3. Indecent Representation of Women (Prohibition) Act (1986) prohibits indecent representation of women through advertisements or in publications, writings, paintings, figures or in any other manner.
4. Commission of Sati (Prevention) Act (1987) provides for the more effective prevention of the commission of sati and its glorification on women.

5. Dowry Prohibition Act (1961) prohibits the giving or taking of dowry at or before or any time after the marriage from women.
6. Maternity Benefit Act (1961) regulates the employment of women in certain establishments for certain period before and after child-birth and provides for maternity benefit and certain other benefits.
7. Medical Termination of Pregnancy Act (1971) provides for the termination of certain pregnancies by registered medical practitioners on humanitarian and medical grounds.
8. Pre-Conception and Pre-Natal Diagnostic Techniques (Prohibition of Sex Selection) Act (1994) prohibits sex selection before or after conception and prevents the misuse of pre-natal diagnostic techniques for sex determination leading to female foeticide.
9. Equal Remuneration Act (1976) provides for payment of equal remuneration to both men and women workers for same work or work of a similar nature. It also prevents discrimination on the ground of sex, against women in recruitment and service conditions.
10. Dissolution of Muslim Marriages Act (1939) grants a Muslim wife the right to seek the dissolution of her marriage.
11. Muslim Women (Protection of Rights on Divorce) Act (1986) protects the rights of Muslim women who have been divorced by or have obtained divorce from their husbands.
12. Family Courts Act (1984) provides for the establishment of Family Courts for speedy settlement of family disputes.
13. Indian Penal Code (1860) contains provisions to protect Indian women from dowry death, rape, kidnapping, cruelty and other offences.
14. Code of Criminal Procedure (1973) has certain safeguards for women like obligation of a person to

maintain his wife, arrest of woman by female police and so on.

15. Indian Christian Marriage Act (1872) contain provisions relating to marriage and divorce among the Christian community.
16. Legal Services Authorities Act (1987) provides for free legal services to Indian women.
17. Hindu Marriage Act (1955) introduced monogamy and allowed divorce on certain specified grounds. It provided equal rights to Indian man and woman in respect of marriage and divorce.
18. Hindu Succession Act (1956) recognizes the right of women to inherit parental property equally with men.
19. Minimum Wages Act (1948) does not allow discrimination between male and female workers or different minimum wages for them.
20. Mines Act (1952) and Factories Act (1948) prohibits the employment of women between 7 P.M. to 6 A.M. in mines and factories and provides for their safety and welfare.
21. The following other legislation's also contain certain rights and safeguards for women:
    1. Employees' State Insurance Act (1948).
    2. Plantation Labour Act (1951).
    3. Bonded Labour System (Abolition) Act (1976).
    4. Legal Practitioners (Women) Act (1923).
    5. Indian Succession Act (1925).
    6. Indian Divorce Act (1869).
    7. Parsi Marriage and Divorce Act (1936).
    8. Special Marriage Act (1954).
    9. Foreign Marriage Act (1969).
    10. Indian Evidence Act (1872).
    11. Hindu Adoptions and Maintenance Act (1956).

22. National Commission for Women Act (1990) provided for the establishment of a National Commission for Women to study and monitor all matters relating to the constitutional and legal rights and safeguards of women.

23. Sexual Harassment of Women at Workplace (Prevention, Prohibition and Redressal). Act (2013) provides protection to women from sexual harassment at all workplaces both in public and private sector, whether organised or unorganized.

Human Rights Management after Globalization **Pages 76-81**
Edited by: Dr. Rabi Narayana Misra
ISBN: 978-93-88854-05-4
Edition: 2019
Published by: Discovery Publishing House Pvt. Ltd., New Delhi (India)

Chapter 8 Development and Human Rights

[1]D.G. Chandrayya
[2]Lt. K. Venkata Rao

Introduction

It has long been accepted by the United Nations and in most international forums that "developed" countries should provide aid in the form of grants and loans to the developing countries. The General Assembly has, by consensus resolutions, called for such development aid to reach 0.7 per cent of the GNP of developed countries. Actually less than half of that target has been attained. For example, the United States gives only less than 0.2 per cent, instead of 0.7 per cent.

Overseas Development Aid (ODA) presents debatable issues from the perspective of human rights. For example, it raises the question whether aid should be directed mainly to reducing poverty and providing social services to the needy or whether priority should be given to economic growth and strengthening infrastructure. Another key question of a legal political characteristic is whether the recipient government or the donor state should have a decisive voice. The developing states emphasize their primary responsibility for development of the country and their right to self-determination in respect of the economy and resources. Donor countries tend to emphasize their narrow concepts of human rights as a prerequisite to sanction development assistance. They also emphasize the pragmatic political fact that aid is not likely to be provided if the beneficiary states violated basic human rights. According

[1] Dept. of Commerce, Kothapeta.
[2] Lecturer in Commerce Government Degree College, Kothapeta, Andhra Pradesh.

to Mikhail Assize, human rights have become another arsenal of Western countries in their bid to bring recalcitrant Third World nations to heel in their New World Order.

The question whether aid should be given to countries where human rights are substantially or systematically violated has been analyzed by Katherine Tomasevski in the following statement.

Donor governments and agencies are continuously making decisions which country to assist, how much and what for, because aid needs are much larger than available aid. Human rights have entered the already numerous criteria for allocating aid fairly recently, this entry has been neither easy nor smooth because no general criteria have been developed by donors and consequently decisions have been made on case-to-case basis. Moreover, these decisions have been limited to some human rights violations in some aid-receiving countries. Thereby human rights terminology has often been used to justify decisions to provide aid or to terminate it; while human rights criteria - to the extent that there is such a thing in the aid policy of any donor - have been confined to the search for those human rights violations which could justify cutting off aid.

Trade and Human Rights

Global trade is being liberalized and opened up in this era of globalization. A set of new rules and regulations have been promoted through international firms like WTO and new initiatives have been taken through the formation of regional economic trading blocs.

At the same time several developed countries in the world have been trying to inter-relate trade policy with human rights policy. Under mounting pressure from the business lobby in the irrespective countries, several Western governments have altered their policies depending up on their business interests. Under the Generalized System of Preferences (GSP) which provides for trade benefits for developing countries, the USA has withdrawn or threatened to withdraw preferences from some countries that violate human rights. The case of China has been controversial, with opinion in the United States sharply divided on the desirability of conditioning trade preferences on compliance with specified human rights. There has been strong pressure from US business lobby against use of the Jackson-Vanik Trade Act of 1974 for denying MFN status to China. It held that talking about "political freedom is not a sound argument for attempting to use the blunt instrument of trade sanctions to win democratic rule for China. Keeping millions of Chinese in poverty by restricting their right to trade, in the hope of promoting human rights, is neither logical nor moral. Likewise, depriving Americans of the freedom to trade and invest in China violates their rights to liberty and property". This is a case of shift in policy based on convenience rather than on ideological convictions or moral principles. On the other hand, some developed countries are pressing for trade sanctions against states found to violate human rights, especially human rights standards that are generally based on the Conventions and Recommendations of the International Labour Organization. They have tended on the whole to oppose trade liberalization treaties such as NAFTA and currently WTO. The developing countries have generally objected to such measures since they would reduce their comparative advantage through cheap labour and constitute a major barrier to their industrialization. From their point of view, workers rights enforced by trade barriers would contribute to greater poverty in their countries.

Drawing on the experience of the "Sullivan Principles" applied by foreign companies operating in South Africa, some activists and scholars have proposed imposing international human rights standards, particularly labour standards, directly on private companies engaged in transnational activity. Guidelines for Multinational Enterprises adopted by the Organization of Economically Developed Countries in 1976 provided for observance of standards of labour relations by transnational companies. A UN Commission on Transnational Corporations devoted about 15 years of study and negotiation on a draft Code of Conduct for Transnational Corporations that included a general provision requiring transnational corporations to respect human rights and fundamental freedoms in the countries where they operate and more detailed provisions on observance of laws on labour relations and involvement of trade unions. Objections of the USA and a few other countries have prevented its adoption. These are some of the examples of the double standards adopted by the developed countries that profess concern for human rights. The fact is that the economically developed countries are in a better position than others to take the advantage of globalization and at the same item dictate policies and guidelines to increase their bargaining power.

The TNCs which have gained strength in the post-globalization era is the main actor in Several developed countries in formulating new foreign policies to shape a new global order. This trend has been highlighted in a recent study that the emerging global order is spearheaded by a few hundred corporate giants, many of them bigger than most sovereign nations. By acquiring earth-spanning technologies, by developing products that can be produced anywhere and sold everywhere, by spreading credit around the world, and by connecting global channels of communication that can penetrate any village or neighbourhood, these institutions we normally think of as economic rather than political, private rather than public, are becoming the world empires of the twenty-first century.

The impact of these global giant's operations have negative impact on human rights. Virtually all developing countries at the present time seek private foreign investment for development. Such investment now greatly exceeds loans or grants from official sources. The growth of Transnational corporations - now numbering about 35,000 with 1,50,000 foreign affiliates - is evidence of the increased role of the private sector and of market economies in developing countries. New technologies have transformed the nature of production and facilitated re-location of firms. Nationalization, once the centre of debate, has now virtually disappeared from the agenda of developing countries.

The human rights implications of these trends are outlined by an economist, David Korten in the following terms:

- Today the most intense competition in the globally integrated market is not between the gigantic Transnational Corporations, but it is between governments that find themselves competing with one another for investors by offering the cheapest and most compliant labour; the weakest environmental, health, and safety standards, the lowest taxes; and the most fully developed infrastructure. Often governments must borrow to finance the social and physical infrastructure needed to attract private investors. Having pushed almost the entire social and environmental costs of production onto the community, many firms are able to turn a handsome profit. Having bargained away their tax base and accepted low wages for their labour, many communities reap relatively few benefits from the foreign investment, however, and are left with no evident way to repay the loans contracted on the firms behalf.[14]

Impact of Globalization on Human Rights

Globalization has its winners and losers. With the expansion of trade, market, foreign investment, developing countries have seen the gaps among themselves widen. The imperative to liberalize has demanded a shrinking of state involvement in national life, producing a wave of privatization, cutting jobs, slashing health, education and food subsidies, etc. affecting the poor people in society. In many cases, liberalization has been accompanied by greater inequality and people are left trapped in utter poverty. Meanwhile, in many industrialized countries unemployment has soared to levels not seen for many years and income disparity to levels not recorded since last century. The collapse of the economies of the Asian Tigers are examples of this. The Human Development Report of 1997 revealed that poor countries and poor people too often find their interests neglected as a result of globalization. Although globalization of the economy has been characterized as a locomotive for productivity, opportunity, technological progress and uniting the world, it ultimately causes increased impoverishment, social disparities and violations of human rights. That is what we see today.

REFERENCES

1. Mohameden Ould-Mey, Global Adjustment; Implications for Peripheral States, Third World Quarterly, 15:2, 1994.
2. Cited in Carole, Collins, A World in Mutation. WSCF Journal, December 1995.
3. Xabier, Gorostiga, Latin America in the New World Order, in Global Visions: Beyond the New World Order, Jeremy Brecher, (ed). (Boston, MA: South end Press, 1993), p.67.
4. Nikhil Aziz, "The Human Rights Debate in an Era of Globalization: Hegemony of Discourse." Bulletin of Concerned Asian Scholars, Vol. 27, No. 4, Oct.-Dec., 1995.
5. International Labour Resource and Information Group, "Getting to Grips with Globalization ", Workers World, No. 3-4, January/February, 1996.
6. Kenichi Ohmae: The End of the Nation State, New York: The Press, 1995. p. 2-5.
7. Robinson Richard and Goodman David S.G. (eds). "The New Rich in Asia: Economic Development, Social Status and Political Consciousness", The New Rich in Asia, London: Routledge. 1996. p. 1.
8. Ohame, op.cit, p. 15.
9. Ibid.
10. Seabrooke Jermey, "Internationalism versus Globalization", Asia-APEC Internet Message, Sept. 11, 1996.
11. Verzola Robert, Asia-APEC internet message, August 6, 1996.
12. Dorn James A, Trade and Human Rights in China, Journal of Commerce, November 15, 1996.
13. Korten David, Sustainable Development: A Review Essay, World Policy Journal, Vol. 9, 157-190.

Human Rights Management after Globalization **Pages 82-99**
Edited by: Dr. Rabi Narayana Misra
ISBN: 978-93-88854-05-4
Edition: 2019
Published by: Discovery Publishing House Pvt. Ltd., New Delhi (India)

Chapter 9

Human Rights in Contemporary India
Issues and Challenges

[1]Dr. B.R. Prasad Reddy
[2]Dr. R.N. Misra

What are Human Rights?

Let's start with the basic meaning of human rights:

Human: A member of the Homo sapiens species; a man, woman or child, a person.

Right: Things to which you are entitled or allowed; freedoms that are guaranteed.

Thus, Human Rights are the rights you have simply because you are human. It is something to which you are entitled by virtue of being human.

If you were to ask people in the street, "What are human rights?" you would get many different answers. They would tell you the rights they know about, but very few people know all their rights. When asked to name their rights, they will list only freedom of speech and belief and perhaps one or two others.

There is no question these are important rights, but the full scope of human rights is very broad:

- They mean choice and opportunity.
- They mean the freedom to obtain a job, adopt a career, select a partner of one's choice and raise children.
- They include the right to travel widely and the right to work gainfully without harassment, abuse and threat of arbitrary dismissal.
- Human interests, needs, reason, autonomy, equality, and capabilities are equally important and universal enough to be protected.

---

[1] Reader in History Government Degree College, Dharmavaram Anantapuramu Dist, A.P.
[2] Prof. MBA, BPUT.

- They even embrace the right to leisure.

Thus, human rights are based on the principle of respect for the individual. Their fundamental assumption is that each person is a moral and rational being who deserves to be treated with dignity. They are called human rights because they are universal. Whereas nations or specialized groups enjoy specific rights that apply only to them, human rights are the rights to which everyone is entitled—no matter who they are or where they live—simply because they are alive.

Evolution of Human Rights

It is generally assumed that the history of Human Rights began with Cyrus Cylinder (539 BCE), which is recognized as the world's first charter of human rights. It is translated into all six official languages of the United Nations and its provisions parallel the first four Articles of the Universal Declaration of Human Rights.

Consequently, documents asserting individual rights, such as the Magna Carta (1215), the Petition of Right (1628), United States Declaration of Independence (1776), the US Constitution (1787), the French Declaration of the Rights of Man and of the Citizen (1789), and the US Bill of Rights (1791) are the written precursors to many of today's human rights documents.

Magna Carta (1215) was a Crucial Turning Point in the Struggle to Establish Freedom

- Gave the right of the church to be free from governmental interference.
- The rights of all free citizens to own and inherit property and to be protected from excessive taxes.
- Established the right of widows who owned property to choose not to remarry.
- Established principles of due process and equality before the law.
- It also contained provisions forbidding bribery and official misconduct.

Petition of Right (1628) asserted four principles:

- No taxes may be levied without consent of Parliament.

- No subject may be imprisoned without cause shown (reaffirmation of the right of habeas corpus).
- No soldiers may be quartered upon the citizenry; and
- Martial law may not be used in time of peace.

United States Declaration of Independence (1776) stressed two themes:

- Individual rights; and
- The right of revolution.

The Constitution of the United States of America *(1787)* protects basic freedoms of US citizens:

It is the oldest written national constitution in use and defines the principal organs of government and their jurisdictions and the basic rights of citizens.

Declaration of the Rights of Man and of the Citizen (1789)

The Declaration by the French first Republic proclaims that all citizens are to be guaranteed the rights of liberty, property, security, and resistance to oppression.

US Bill of Rights (1791) limited the powers of the federal government of the US and protected the rights of all citizens:

- Protected freedom of speech, freedom of religion, the right to keep and bear arms, the freedom of assembly and the freedom to petition.
- Protected unreasonable search and seizure, cruel and unusual punishment and compelled self-incrimination.
- Prohibited Congress from making any law respecting establishment of religion.
- Prohibited the federal government from depriving any person of life, liberty or property without due process of law.

The Universal Declaration of Human Rights (1948)

In the wake of immeasurable destruction and devastation caused by 2nd World War, fifty nations met in San Francisco in 1945 and formed the United Nations to protect and promote peace. By 1948, the United Nations' new Human Rights

Commission had captured the world's attention. Under the chairmanship of Eleanor Roosevelt—President Franklin Roosevelt's widow, a human rights champion in her own right and the United States delegate to the UN—the Commission set out to draft the document that became the Universal Declaration of Human Rights asserting that "all human beings are born free and equal in dignity and rights." In its preamble and in Article 1, the Declaration unequivocally proclaims the inherent rights of all human beings.

Roosevelt, credited with its inspiration, referred to the Declaration as the international Magna Carta for all mankind. ***It was adopted by the United Nations on December 10, 1948.*** The Universal Declaration of Human Right has inspired a number of other human rights laws and treaties throughout the world.

The Member States of the United Nations pledged to work together to promote the thirty Articles of human rights that, for the first time in history, had been assembled and codified into a single document. In consequence, many of these rights, in various forms, are today part of the constitutional laws of democratic nations.

Thirty Articles of Human Rights are:

1. We Are All Born Free & Equal
2. Don't Discriminate
3. The Right to Life
4. No Slavery
5. No Torture
6. You Have Rights No Matter Where You Go
7. We're All Equal Before the Law
8. Your Human Rights Are Protected by Law
9. No Unfair Detainment
10. The Right to Trial
11. We're Always Innocent Till Proven Guilty
12. The Right to Privacy
13. Freedom to Move

14. The Right to Seek a Safe Place to Live
15. Right to a Nationality
16. Marriage and Family
17. The Right to Your Own Things
18. Freedom of Thought
19. Freedom of Expression
20. The Right to Public Assembly
21. The Right to Democracy
22. Social Security
23. Workers' Rights
24. The Right to Play
25. Food and Shelter for All
26. The Right to Education
27. Copyright
28. A Fair and Free World
29. Responsibility
30. No One Can Take Away Your Human Rights.

At this juncture, let have a look at the issue of fundamental rights and human rights. Sometimes fundamental and human rights do overlap as the latter serves as foundation to the former. The issue of context cannot be removed in the determination of fundamental rights but human rights enjoy a sort of universal context. For example the right to live is universal but the right to live in a state is fundamental according to the rules set up by the state to guide such right.

Fundamental Rights Vs. Human Rights

Fundamental Rights	Human Rights
• Fundamental rights are rights and freedoms guaranteed by constitutions of some countries of the world to their citizens (country specific).	• Human rights are designed in such a way that they are of even more basic nature and apply to all human beings across the world without any discrimination.

• These rights have a legal sanction and can be challenged by affected individuals in a court of law.	• Human rights do not have such sanctity and are not enforceable in courts.
• Among these rights are the right to life, liberty (of freedom, free will and personal), pursuit of happiness, and so on.	• The right to a dignified human life is one such human right which cannot be questioned whether you are in US or in a poor African country.
• These rights are considered to be the most basic rights and are provided to all citizens of the country without any discrimination.	• No consensus on universal human rights.
• There are other fundamental rights such as the right to profess faith, right to movement across the country, right to freedom of speech and belief.	
Fundamental Rights = Rights being a citizen Being	**Human Rights = Rights being a Human Being**

Status of Human Rights in India

- Demonetization
- Armed Forces Special Powers Act (AFSPA)
- Lynching of Aklaq Ahmad
- Triple talaaq
- Perumal Murugan, author of Madhorubagan announces his death as writer
- Rohit Vemula's suicide
- Clamping of Sedition cases etc. ......

"Many people are not aware that there are human rights violations right here in India and they occur daily among socially marginalized sections: discrimination, human trafficking, domestic violence, minority baiting, maltreatment of children, environmental degradation, forcible land acquisition and the list goes on...

Many Western scholars with their colonial and missionary background claim that the concept of human rights is a Western concept but they are not absolutely right. The universality of human rights is based on the universal values prevalent in all the major civilizations of the world. Indian culture also has evolved from time to time some great notions of human rights and duties.

Some Vedic concepts suggests human beings certain rights and responsibilities. Though securing rights and fighting to protect them are not mentioned explicitly the Vedic literature of India, Indian culture is not inimical to human rights.

'No one is superior or inferior; all are brothers; all should strive for the interest of all and progress collectively'. *Ajyesthaaso Akanisthaasa Yete - Sam Bhraataro Vaavrudhuh Soubhagaya, RigVeda, Mandala-5, Sukta-60, Mantra-5*

Regarding the rights of women in India, Prof. H.H. Wilson says: "It may be confidently asserted that in no nation of antiquity were women held in so much esteem as amongst Hindus". (Mill's *History ofBharat,* Vol. II)

Manu Smriti, the greatest work on Hindu social codes, declares: *Yatra Naryastu Pujyante Ramante Tatra Devatah* - "Where women are worshipped there the angels tread".

It defined the status of a wife and her equal rights thus:

1. If a wife dies, her husband may marry another wife. *(Manu,* Chapter V, Verse 168). If a husband dies, a wife may marry another husband. *(Manu,* quoted by Madhava and Vidyanatha Dikshita; Parasara; Narada; Yagnavalkya; Agni Purana).
2. If a wife becomes fallen by drunkenness or immorality her husband may marry another. *(Manu,* Chapter IX,

Verse 80). If a husband becomes fallen, a wife may re-marry another husband. (*Manu,* quoted by Madhava and several other scholars).

3. In particular circumstances, a wife may cease to cohabit with her husband. (*Manu,* Chapter IX, Verse 79).
4. If a husband deserts his wife, she may marry another. (*Manu,* Chapter IX, Verse 76 and several others).

The above discussion has been attempted to encourage debate, discuss and have a general exchange of ideas. However, the human rights issue has taken a serious turn in the 20th century.

A number of social movements have marked Indian history from the 1800s onwards. The Indian Civil Liberties Union (ICLU) was established in 1934, the first civil rights organization in India. Its main activities were gathering information about violations of civil liberties, particularly regarding the conditions of prisoners and people in detention, police brutality, proscriptions on literature and restrictions on the press. Along with the ICLU, the Bombay Civil Liberties Union, the Madras Civil Liberties Union, and the Punjab Civil Liberties Union further strengthened the rights movements.

After independence, the government's commitment to civil liberties was challenged by left-wing Naxalite movement and this resulted in severe violation of human rights during 1960s. During 1975-76 when a nation-wide state of emergency was imposed, the human rights movement developed a wide organizational base and became more visible. Several organizations like People's Union for Civil Liberties and Democratic Rights, the Andhra Pradesh Civil Liberties Union, and the Association for the Protection of Democratic Rights were formed. At present People's Union for Civil Liberties, People's Union for Democratic Rights, Child Rights and You, APCLC, Human Rights Forum, Bachpan Bacho Andolan, Vigil Indian Movement, Love Commandos, MRPS etc. are very active.

Major Activities Taken up by These Groups, Namely:

- Fact-finding missions and investigations
- Public interest litigation
- Citizen awareness programme
- Campaigns
- Production of supportive literature for independent movements and organizations.

Despite severe restrictions, the human rights movement has been able to assure freer and fairer elections today by way of a more informed electorate; to pressure the government to give access to international organizations like Amnesty International; to establish NHRC etc.

National Human Rights Commission in India

The National Human Rights Commission in India was established in 1993. According to the Protection of Human Rights Act, 1993, under which the national and state human rights commissions are constituted, the NHRC Chairperson has to be a former CJI. The President appoints the chairperson and other members of the NHRC on the recommendations of the committee, which also includes the Lok Sabha Speaker, the Home Minister, leaders of the Opposition in the Lok Sabha and the Rajya Sabha, and the deputy chairperson of the Rajya Sabha.

The main task assigned to NHRC is to inquire, *suo motu* or on a petition presented to it by a victim or any person on his behalf. It can be on the direction or order of any court to look into the complaint of violation of human rights.

The post of Chairperson at NHRC, which has been lying vacant since May 11, 2016 when Shri Justice K G Balakrishnan demitted office after completing his five-year term, is filled with Shri Justice Dattu on 29/02/2016. The delay in appointment of the NHRC chairman does have a direct bearing on the administration of justice and the rule of law.

In fact, the Preamble, Part III of the Constitution consisting of Fundamental Rights, Part IV comprising Directive Principles and Part IV (A) containing Fundamental Duties, constitute the human rights framework which was heavily influenced by the UDHR. However, none of the rights are absolute, and are subject to 'reasonable restriction' in the larger interest of the community as well as of the State.

India has taken important strides in recent years, in particular with legal reform with respect to the treatment of Dalits, women and various vulnerable groups:

- In 2015, the government enacted the Scheduled Castes and Scheduled Tribes (Prevention of Atrocities) Amendment Bill, strengthening protections for Dalit and tribal communities, and making it easier for them to pursue justice.
- More recently, the government has introduced a "transgender person bill" that, although it needs refinement and further input from civil society, is a good step toward protecting and empowering the country's transgender population.
- There is also a Mental Health Care Bill and Rights of Persons with Disabilities Bill pending in parliament, aimed at advancing the rights of people with disabilities.
- There was encouraging progress on security force accountability in 2015, with the army confirming life imprisonment for six soldiers for a 2010 extra judicial killing of three villagers in the Machil sector in Jammu and Kashmir states. The rare guilty verdict was delivered by a military court in November 2014 and was confirmed in September 2015 *(However, the government failed to repeal laws that provide public officials and security forces immunity from prosecution for abuses without prior authorization. Lack of progress in implementing long-overdue police reforms showed the unwillingness among public officials to make the force more accountable and free from political interference).*

But in many areas, the government and local authorities continue to fall short, both with respect to legal reforms and implementation.

Human Rights Violations in India in Recent Times

Human rights advocates agree that, sixty nine years after its issue, the Universal Declaration of Human Rights is still more a dream than reality. Violations exist in every part of the world and India unfortunately is not an exception:

- 70% of Indian wealth is owned by 57 people ***(in the last two decades 10% of top wealthy Indian acquired*** 15% ***of properties; while the poorest 10% lost their*** 15% ***earnings).***
- Tribals of Chinna Jaggampeta in Nathavaram mandal of Visakhapatnam district left to starve by ruthorities, this January (2017) over a 22-acre piece of land.
- In October, 2016 around 30 Maoists were killed in Andhra Orissa border.
- In April, 2015 police killed 20 men in the forests of Andhra Pradesh, alleging they were smugglers and claiming they fired in self-defense. On the same day, five terrorism suspects in Telangana state were killed in custody as they were being transported from jail for a court hearing. Investigations are pending in both cases; rights groups say there is evidence that police staged both sets of killings.
- In May, 2015 the northeastern state of Tripura revoked the draconian Armed Forces Special Powers Act (AFSPA), citing a decline in insurgency. However, it remains in force in Jammu and Kashmir and in other northeastern states. A May report by the United Nations special reporter on extrajudicial, summary, or arbitrary executions noted that "impunity remains a serious problem" and expressed regret that India had not repealed or at least radically amended AFSPA.
- In 2014 and 2015, several police officials were reinstated in Gujarat despite having been implicated in the alleged 2004 "encounter" killing of 19-year-old Ishrat Jahan and three others, raising concerns about the government's commitment to police accountability.

- Violence against women, particularly rape and murder, made headlines throughout 2016. While legal reforms in the form of NIRBHAYA ACT introduced in response to the 2012 Delhi gang rape and murder gave prosecutors new tools for pursuing such crimes, they also expanded use of the death penalty. The Indian government does not appear to have a mechanism in place to track the efficacy of the reforms in preventing and punishing sexual violence. It has also failed to take effective measures to reduce sexual harassment and improve women's access to safe transportation.
- In August, village leaders in Uttar Pradesh state allegedly ordered the rape of two Dalit sisters to pay for the "sins" of their brother who had eloped with a higher-caste woman. These unofficial village councils, called *Khaps,* made up of men from dominant castes who often enjoy political patronage, are known to issue edicts restricting women's mobility and rights, and condemning couples for marrying outside their caste or religion.
- *Child Rights:* Recently, the lower house of parliament passed amendments to the Juvenile Justice Act to permit prosecution of 16 and 17-year-olds in adult court when charged with serious crimes such as rape and murder. A parliamentary standing committee, children's rights activists, and the National Commission for Protection of Child Rights all strongly oppose the amendments as this would prohibit most employment of children under 14, but would permit them to work in family enterprises after school hours. This amendment, in the absence of effective implementation of the right to education law, could actually push more children into child labour.
- *Sexual Orientation and Gender Identity:* LGBT individuals continue to face harassment, extortion, intimidation, and abuse, including by the police. In December 2013, the Supreme Court upheld the constitutionality of

section 377 of the Indian penal code, which criminalizes same-sex conduct between consenting adults. In 2014, the Supreme Court mandated legal recognition of transgender people as a third gender and ruled them beligible for special education and employment benefits. The parliament is attending to frame an act in this regard.

- *Restrictions on Free Speech:* Authorities regularly uses India's sedition law and criminal defamation law to prosecute citizens who criticize government officials. Kanhaiya Kumar, a student union leader at the J. N. University was one of those arrested for sedition. In several cases, interest groups that claimed to be offended by books, movies, or works of art pushed for censorship or harassed authors.
- Recently a Tamil author decided to give up his writing career after being coerced by state authorities to tender an unconditional apology to calm down angry mobs unhappy with one of his books.
- In Tamil Nadu, police arrested a folk singer under the sedition law for two songs that criticized the state government.
- Gujarat police arrested Hardik Patel, who is spearheading protests to demand quotas in education and government jobs for his community, and charged him with sedition in two separate cases.
- Khurram Parvez, a human rights activist was detained in his home on September 15, 2016, in Kashmir and stopped him from traveling to the United Nations Human Rights Council in Geneva.
- However, fortunately in a big win for online expression, the Supreme Court struck down section 66A of the Information Technology Act, which criminalized a broad range of speech and had been used by authorities to pursue critics of the government.

- *Civil Society and Freedom of Association:* Authorities intensified their crackdown on civil society by using the Foreign Contribution Regulation Act (FCRA), a law regulating grants from foreign donors, to harass organizations that questioned or criticized government policies. The government cut off funds to organizations, including Greenpeace India, and put restrictions on others, including the Ford Foundation.
- Authorities labeled activists "anti-national" when they questioned government infrastructure and development projects or sought justice for victims of the 2002 communal riots in Gujarat. Such tactics had a chilling effect on the work of other groups.
- Government targeted activist Teesta Setalvad and her husband, Javed Anand, in what appeared to be acts of politically motivated intimidation, accusing them of violating the FCRA and receiving funds illegally, among other allegations. The government suspended the registration of their organization, the Sabrang Trust, under the FCRA, and moved to cancel the license. Setalvad is well-known for her work supporting victims of the 2002 Gujarat riots and for seeking criminal charges against scores of officials, including Prime Minister Modi for his alleged involvement in the riots as the state's then chief minister.
- The government in 2015 put the Ford Foundation on a FCRA watchlist, requiring the foundation to get prior approval from the government for all its programmatic activities in India—an action almost certainly linked to Ford's funding of Teesta Setalvad's organization, Sabrang.
- The government barred Priya Pillai, a Greenpeace India activist, from boarding a flight to London where she was to speak to members of the British Parliament, alleging that her testimony would have portrayed the government in a negative light abroad at a time when it was looking to attract foreign investment. Authorities in

Tamil Nadu, where Greenpeace India's registered office is located, cancelled the organization's registration.

- Most recently, the government has initiated investigation of two well-known lawyers, Indira Jaising, a former Additional Solicitor General, and her husband, Anand Grover, a former UN Special Rapporteur on the right to health. On May 31, 2016 the government temporarily suspended the FCRA status of the Lawyers Collective, an organization founded by Grover and Jaising, citing alleged violations under the FCRA. Many believe that the focus on the Lawyers Collective is politically motivated and that the government is attempting to disempower and weaken them because of their work in assisting and supporting Priya Pillai of Greenpeace India and Teesta Setalvad. Jaising and **Grover have also routinely represented people in cases against the current government, as well as the president of the ruling party, Amit Shah, protesting his discharge in an alleged case of extrajudicial killing.**
- Prolonged pre-trial detention and overcrowding in jails remained widespread. As of January, 2014 over 282,000 prisoners - 68% of the total prison population - were pre-trial detainees. Dalits, Adivasis and Muslims continued to be disproportionately represented.
- A 2014 Supreme Court order directing district judges to release pre-trial detainees who had been held for over half of the term they would have served if convicted was poorly implemented.
- *Corporate Accountability:* In February, the government introduced a bill to amend India's land acquisition law which removed requirements related to obtaining consent and conducting impact assessments for a range of industrial projects. Following nationwide opposition from farmers' groups, civil society and political parties, the government said in August that it would not pursue the amendments. Many industries, including public sector coal mines, railways and highways, were

still not required to obtain the consent of Indigenous communities or conduct social impact assessments.

- Vulnerable communities in resource-rich areas remained at risk of forced evictions. The Environment Ministry sought to abolish a requirement for consent from village assemblies for certain infrastructure projects. The list goes on and on........

Challenges

While the human rights movement in India has been successful in mitigating some serious forms of oppression, and has kept alive the spirit of democracy in India, it is not without its limitations:

- Most of the organizations are voluntary in nature.
- Based on individual or collective enthusiasm for special interests.
- Not based on all-encompassing rights foundations.
- State's repression and counter attack through Government Organized Non-Governmental, Organizations (GONGOs) (these are very aggressive and create confusion).
- Civil society groups faced increased harassment and government critics faced intimidation and lawsuits.
- NGO sector has become politicized.
- Explosion of NGOs - many are inefficient and corrupt.
- Criticism that many NGOs are largely Western in origin and conception.
- Poor or inaccurate research.
- Bias reporting.
- Instead of resolving the crisis - enhances in certain cases.

Remedies

- To make citizenry conscious and vigilant.
- To increase public participation in the movement.

- To resolve conflict between the NGOs and the State.
- To not harp on history; understand history.
- To safeguard human rights and to prevent the State from encroaching on the same.
- To incorporate Human Rights education into our children's curriculum. They must know their human rights to be aware of human rights violations.
- To arrest environmental degradation at the local and global level.
- To entitle water and sanitation to everyone as it is a basic human right.

Current Major Areas of Research Related to Human Rights

Researchers are currently working on exciting empirical and normative aspects of human rights. The scholars are asking questions such as:

- Why do some political regimes torture, whereas others do not?
- Why do some people commit genocide, crimes against humanity, or war crimes?
- Why are some countries democratic, whereas others are not?
- What is a human right and how do we know what should be included in a list of human rights?
- Who has the responsibilities to guarantee human rights?
- Which human right matters first - the substantive (socio-economic, i.e. the right to health, food security, literacy, job) right or civil and political right (*i.e.* liberty, speech, property)?

Despite the cry after the Holocaust of "never again," genocides, war crimes, crimes against humanity and other widespread human rights failures continue to occur practically worldwide. Much more scholarly research, as well as practical invention and creativity is needed in order to make progress on preventing these atrocities.

Conclusion

Human rights exist, as embodied in the Universal Declaration of Human Rights and the entire body of international human rights law. They are recognized—rat least in principle—by most nations and form the heart of many national constitutions. Yet the actual situation in the world is far distant from the ideals envisioned in the Declaration.

To some, the full realization of human rights is a remote and unattainable goal. Even international human rights laws are difficult to enforce and pursuing a complaint can take years and a great deal of money. These international laws serve as a restraining function but are insufficient to provide adequate human rights protection, as evidenced by the stark reality of abuses perpetrated daily.

But you can make a difference. Become informed by reading the reports on human rights around the world and do your bit.

REFERENCES

1. South Asia Human Rights Documentation Centre, New Delhi Newspapers.
2. Interaction with Human Rights Forum Activists & Police Officers.

Human Rights Management after Globalization **Pages 100-110**
Edited by: Dr. Rabi Narayana Misra
ISBN: 978-93-88854-05-4
Edition: 2019
Published by: Discovery Publishing House Pvt. Ltd., New Delhi (India)

Chapter 10 Women Empowerment in India

[1]Dr. Brajamohan Sasmal

Introduction

As we all know that India is a male dominated country where males are dominated in every area and females are forced to be responsible for only family care and live within the four walls of the home with many social restrictions. Almost 50% of the population in India is covered by the female only, so the full development of the country also depends on the other half of the population, means, women, who are not empowered and still restricted by many social barriers. In such condition, we cannot say that our country would be the fully, developed in the future without empowering its other half of the population, means women. If we want to make our country a fully developed country first of all it is very necessary to empower women by the efforts of men, government policies and Acts and women themselves too.

Women empowerment can be defined in very simple words that it is making women powerful so that they can take their own decisions regarding their lives and well being in the family and society. It is empowering women to make them able to get their real rights in the society. According to the United Nations, women's empowerment mainly has five components:

- Generating women's sense of self- worth;
- Women's right to have and to determine their choices;

[1] Retd. Prof. of Chemistry, Berhampur-760001.

- Women's right to have access to equal opportunities and all kinds of resources;
- Women's right to have the power to regulate and control their own lives, within and outside the home; and
- Women's ability to contribute in creating a more just social and economic order.

Thus, women empowerment is nothing but recognition of women's basic human rights and creating an environment where they are treated as equals to men.

Need of Women Empowerment

The need of women empowerment arose because of the gender discrimination and male domination in the Indian society since ancient time. Women are being suppressed by their family members and society for many reasons. They have been targeted for many types of violence and discriminatory practices by the male members in the family and society in India and other countries as well. Wrong and old practices for the women in the society from ancient time have taken the form of well developed customs and traditions. There is a tradition of worshipping many female goddesses in India including giving honour to the women forms in the society like mother, sister, daughter, wife and other female relatives or friends. But, it does not mean that only respecting or honouring women can fulfil the need of development in the country. It needs the empowerment of the rest, half population of the country in every walk of life.

India is a famous country proving the common proverb like 'unity is diversity', where people of many religious beliefs are in the Indian society. Women have been given a special place in every religion which is working as a big curtain covering the eyes of people and help in the continuation of many ill practices (including physical and mental) against women as a norm since ages. In the ancient Indian society, there was a custom of sati pratha, nagar vadhu system, dowry system, sexual violence, domestic violence, female infanticide, parda pratha, wife burning, sexual harassment at workplace, child marriage, child labour, devadashi pratha, etc. including other discriminatory practices.

All such type of ill practices, is against women because of male superiority complex and orthodox mentality of the society.

Even in this 21st century Gender inequality still exists.

There are so many women, who are silently bearing the harassment of their life partners because of the lack of education, lack of legal awareness and lack of empowerment:

- When women are empowered, whole society benefits.
- Educating women about health care promotes healthier families.
- Even though a woman works 24/7 hours a week to raise her children and to maintain her family, she is not getting recognition for the work.
- "There is no chance of the welfare of the world unless the condition of women is improved. It is not possible for a bird to fly on one wing." - Swami Vivekananda.
- Women's empowerment is needed in order to check the following misdeeds caused by our society such as:
  Female Foeticide, Dowry Demands, Restriction on widow remarriage, Gender Bias, Neglect during Childhood, Childhood marriages, Gender specific specialization at work, Cultural definition of appropriate gender roles, Belief in the inherent superiority of males. Families are considered as a private sphere and stays under male control, Limited access to cash and credit, Limited employment opportunities, Limited access to education, Female infanticide, Poverty effects women more than men, India's maternal mortality is highest in South Asia, Domestic violence, Crimes against women, Honor killings, Trafficking of women, Lack of awareness about government schemes.

Possibility of Empowerment of Women In India

Socio-political rights such as right to work, right to education, right to decide for themselves, etc. for the women were completely restricted by the male members of family. Some of the ill practices against women have been eliminated by the open minded and great Indian people who raise their voices for the discriminatory practices against women. Through the continuous efforts of the Raja Ram Mohan Roy, Britshers were forced to eliminate the ill practice of Sati paratha. Later, other famous social reformers of the India like Ishwar Chandra Vidyasagar, Acharya Vinoba Bhave, Swami Vivekananda, etc. also had raised their voices and worked hard for the upliftment of women in Indian society. In India, the Widow Remarriage Act, 1856 was initiated by the continuous efforts of Ishwar Chandra Vidyasagar in order to improve the conditions of widows in the country.

In the recent years, various constitutional and legal rights have been implemented by the Government of India in order to eliminate ill practices and gender discrimination against women. However, in order to solve such a big issue, the continuous effort of everyone including women is required. Modern society is being more aware about the women rights which results in the increasing number of several self-help groups, NGOs, etc. working in this direction. Women are being more open minded and breaking the societal barriers in order to achieve their rights in all dimensions even after crimes are going side by side.

Some of the acts passed by the Parliament are Equal Remuneration Act, 1976, Dowry Prohibition Act-1961, Immoral Traffic (Prevention) Act-1956, Medical termination of Pregnancy Act, 1971, Maternity Benefit Act, 1961, Commission of Sati (Prevention) Act, 1987, Prohibition of Child Marriage Act, 2006, Pre-Conception & Pre-Natal Diagnostic Techniques (Regulation and; Prevention of Misuse) Act-1994, Sexual Harassment of Women at Workplace (Prevention, Protection and) Act, 2013, etc. in order to empower women with legal rights. In order to provide safety to women and reduce crime against women in India, government has passed another act Juvenile Justice (Care and Protection of Children) Bill, 2015 (especially after Nirbhaya case when an accused juvenile was released). This act is the replacement earlier Indian juvenile delinquency law of 2000, Juvenile Justice (Care and Protection of Children) Act, 2000) in order to reduce the juvenile age from 18 to 16 years in cases of heinous offenses.

Attempts Made for Empowerment of Women by Indian Government

A. Government Acts:

Section 14 of the Hindu Succession Act, 1956—Property of a female Hindu to be her absolute property.

Hindu Succession (Amendment) Act, 2005—Women get equal share in the ancestral property.

- Dowry prohibition Act, 1961.
- ***Contract Labour Act, 1970 & Factories Act, 1948***- Women can't be employed in the night between 9 pm to 6 am — Women cannot be required to work for more than 9 hrs.
- Equal remuneration Act, 1976.
- The indecent representation of women (prohibition) Act, 1986.
- Commission of Sati (Prevention) Act, 1987.
- Protection of women from domestic violence Act, 2005.
- Maternity Benefits Act, 1961.
- Child Marriage (Prohibition) Act, 1929.
- ***Hindu Marriage Act, 1955***— This act was passed to stop polygamy and bigamy.

B. Government Schemes and Programs

STEP (Support to training-cum-Employment for women)- To increase the self-reliance and autonomy of women by enhancing their productivity & enabling them to take up income generation activity:

- ***SSA (Sarva Shiksha Abhiyan)***—For girl child education. It lead to increase in the Gender Parity Index (GPI).
- ***The National Literacy Mission or Saakshar Bharat***— Literacy of women. Literacy is the critical instrument of women's empowerment.
- ***National Rural Health Mission***—Educating women on health care. It has resulted in the decline in fertility rates, Maternal Mortality Rates (MMR), Infant Mortality Rates (IMR).
- ***SHG (Self Help Groups)***—For economic development in women by giving micro finances.

- ***GB (Gender Budgeting)***—Identifying the felt needs of women and reprioritizing and increasing expenditure to meet these needs.
- ***NMEW (National Mission for Empowerment of Women)***—To ensure economic & social empowerment of women.
- ***Swayamsidha Scheme***—To ensures total development of women.
- ***Swadhar Scheme***—Basic necessities to marginalized women & girls.
- ***Kishori Shakti Yojana***—Empowerment of adoiscent girls.
- ***Mahila Samridhi Yojana***—For women empowerment.
- ***Maternity Benefit Scheme***—Payment of ₹ 500 to pregnant women for the first two births only if the woman belongs to BPL (Below Poverty Line) category.
- ***Rastriya Mahila Kosh***—To provide micro loans for women.
- ***Scheme for working women hostel***—To promote availability of safe & conveniently located accommodation for working women.
- ***Development of women & children in Rural Areas (DWCRA)***—Creation of groups of women for income generating activities on self-sustaining basis.
- ***SABLA***—Empowerment of adolescent girls.

C. Preamble to the Constitution

The Preamble to the Constitution of India assures justice, social, economic and political; equality of status and opportunity and dignity to the individual. Thus it treats both men and women equal.

The policy of women empowerment is well entreflipd in the Fundamental Rights enshrined in our Constitution. For example:

- Article 14 ensures to women the right to equality.

- Article 15(1) specifically prohibits discrimination on the basis of sex.
- Article 15(3) empowers the State to take affirmative actions in favour of women.
- Article 16 provides for equality of opportunity for all citizens in matters relating to employment or appointment to any office.

These rights being fundamental rights which are justiciable in court and the Government is obliged to follow the same.

D. Directive Principles of State Policy

Directive principles of State Policy also contains important provisions, regarding women empowerment and it is the duty of the government to apply these principles while making laws or formulating any policy. Though these are not justiciable in the Court but these are essential for governance nonetheless. Some of them are:

- Article 39 (a) provides that the State to direct its policy towards securing for men and women equally the right to an adequate means of livelihood.
- Article 39 (d) mandates equal pay for equal work for both men and women.
- Article 42 provides that the State to make provision for securing just and humane conditions of work and for maternity relief.

The Fundamental duties are enshrined in Part TV-A of the Constitution and are positive duties for the people of India to follow. It also contains a duty related to women's rights: Article 51 (A) (e) expects from the citizen of the country to promote harmony and the spirit of common brotherhood amongst all the people of India and to renounce practices derogatory to the dignity of women.

E. Other Constitutional Provisions

Through 73rd and 74th Constitutional Amendment of 1993, a very, important political right has been given to women which is a landmark in the direction of women empowerment in India. With this amendment women were given 33.33 per cent reservation in seats at different levels of elections in local governance *i.e.* at Panchayat, Block and Municipality elections. Thus it can be seen that these Constitutional provisions are very empowering for women and the State is duty bound to apply these principles in taking policy decisions as well as in enacting law. Given below:

Here is the list of some specific laws which were enacted by the Parliament in order to fulfil Constitutional obligation of women empowerment:

- The Equal Remuneration Act, 1976.
- The Dowry Prohibition Act, 1961.
- The Immoral Traffic (Prevention) Act, 1956.
- The Maternity Benefit Act, 1961.
- The Medical Termination of Pregnancy Act, 1971.
- The Commission of Sati (Prevention) Act, 1987.
- The Prohibition of Child Marriage Act, 2006.
- The Pre-Conception & Pre-Natal Diagnostic Techniques (Regulation and Prevention of Misuse) Act, 1994.
- The Sexual Harassment of Women at Workplace (Prevention, Protection) Act, 2013.

Above mentioned and several other laws are there which not only provide specific legal rights to women but also gives them a sense of security and empowerment.

V. Government Policies and Schemes for Women Empowerment

Whatever improvement and empowerment women have received is especially due to their own efforts and struggle, though governmental schemes are also there to help them in their endeavour. In the year 2001, the Government of India launched a National Policy for Empowerment of Women. The specific objectives of the policy are as follows:

- Creation of an environment through positive economic and social policies for full development of women to enable them to realize their full potential.

- Creation of an environment for enjoyments of all human rights and fundamental freedom by women on equal basis with men in all political, economic, social, cultural and civil spheres.
- Providing equal access to participation and decision making of women in social political and economic life of the nation.
- Providing equal access to women to health care, quality education at all levels, career and vocational guidance, employment, equal remuneration, occupational health and safety, social security and public life etc.
- Strengthening legal systems aimed at elimination of all forms of discrimination against women.
- Changing societal attitudes and community practices by active participation and involvement of both men and women.
- Mainstreaming a gender perspective in the development process.
- Elimination of discrimination and all forms of violence against women and the girl child.
- Building and strengthening partnerships with civil society, particularly women's organizations.

The Ministry of Women and Child Development is the nodal agency for all matters pertaining to welfare, development and empowerment of women. It has evolved schemes and programmes for their benefit. These schemes are spread across a very wide spectrum such as women's need for shelter, security, safety, legal aid, justice, information, maternal health, food, nutrition etc., as well as their need for economic sustenance through skill development, education and access to credit and marketing.

Various schemes of the Ministry are like Swashakti, Swayamsidha, STEP and Swawlamban enable economic empowerment. Working Women Hostels and Creches provide support services. Swadhar and Short Stay Homes provide protection and rehabilitation to women in difficult circumstances. The Ministry also supports autonomous bodies like National Commission, Central Social Welfare Board and Rashtriya Mahila Kosh which work for the welfare and development of women. Economic sustenance of women through skill development, education and access to credit and marketing is also one of the areas where the Ministry has special focus.

VI. International Commitments of India as to Women Empowerment

India is a part to various International conventions and treaties which are committed to secure equal rights of women. One of the most important among them is the Convention on Elimination of All Forms of Discrimination against Women (CEDAW), ratified by India in 1993. Other important International instruments for women empowerment are: The Mexico Plan of Action (1975), the Nairobi Forward Looking Strategies (1985), the Beijing Declaration as well as the Platform for Action (1995) and the Outcome Document adopted by the UNGA Session on Gender Equality and Development & Peace for the 21st century, titled "Further actions and initiatives to implement the Beijing Declaration and the Platform for Action". All these have been whole-heartedly endorsed by India for appropriate follow up.

These various national and International commitments, laws and policies notwithstanding women's situation on the ground have still not improved satisfactorily. Varied problems related to women are still subsisting; female infanticide is growing, dowry is still prevalent, domestic violence against women is practised; sexual harassment at workplace and other heinous sex crimes against women are on the rise.

Though, economic and social condition of women has improved in a significant way but the change is especially visible only in metro cities or in urban areas; the situation is not much improved in semi-urban areas and villages. This disparity is due to lack of education and job opportunities and negative mind set of the society which does not approve girls'education even in 21st century.

VII. Conclusion and Suggestions

In conclusion, it can be said that women in India, through their own unrelenting efforts and with the help of Constitutional and other legal provisions and also with the aid of Government's various welfare schemes, are trying to find their own place under the sun. And it is a heartening sign that their participation in employment-government as well as private, in socio-political Activities of the nation and also their presence at the highest decision-making bodies is improving day by day.

Women should do self help for their own empowerment as suggested below:

- First of all, woman must have the will to be independent & to be the best of - herself, then rest of everything follows.
- Creating legal aweness among women about their rights.
- Educating women. Education makes them independent.
- Providing health facilities & economic security.
- Skill development programmes.
- Forming groups. Unity gives strength to everyone.
- And many more little things which makes significant difference and leads to the great future.

However, we are still far behind in achieving the equality and justice which the Preamble of our Constitution talks about. The real problem lies in the patriarchal and male-dominated system of our society which considers women as subordinate to men and creates different types of methods to subjugate them.

The need of us is to educate and sensitize male members of the society regarding women issues and try to inculcate a feeling of togetherness and equality among them so that they would stop their discriminatory practices towards the fairer sex.

For this to happen apart from Government, the efforts are needed from various NGOs and from enlightened citizens of the country. And first of all efforts should begin from our homes where we must empower female members of our family by providing them equal opportunities of education, health, nutrition and decision making without any discrimination.

Because India can become a powerful nation only if it truly empowers its women.

Human Rights Management after Globalization **Pages 111-122**
Edited by: Dr. Rabi Narayana Misra
ISBN: 978-93-88854-05-4
Edition: 2019
Published by: Discovery Publishing House Pvt. Ltd., New Delhi (India)

Chapter 11

Child Labour in India

A Human Rights Perspective

[1]Dr. P. Shanmukha Rao

Introduction

Child labour is undoubtedly a human rights issue. It is not only exploitative but also endangers children's physical, cognitive, emotional, social, and moral development. It perpetuates poverty because a child labour, deprived of education or healthy physical development, is likely to become an adult with low earning prospects. This is a vicious cycle which apart from ruining the lives of many results in an overall backwardness in the masses.

Moreover, conceptualising child labour as a human rights issue gives the victim with the authority to hold violators liable. Human rights generate legal grounds for political activity and expression, because they entail greater moral force than ordinary legal obligations. Children are right holders with the potential to make valuable contributions to their own present and future well being as well as to the social and economic development of the society and thus they should under no circumstances be perceived as passive and vulnerable.

Today, traditionally prescribed interventions against child labour which were welfare based like providing a minimum age for work are being replaced by rights-based approach. A rights-based approach to child labour needs to be adopted which puts internationally recognized rights of children to the center while utilizing UDHR, ICCPR and ICESCR as a supportive framework. Child labour is a condition from which

[1] Department of Commerce Government College (A) Rajamundry, Andhra Pradesh

the children have a right to be free and it is not merely an option for which regulating standards must be devised.

A Human Rights Approach to Child Labour

Initially, scholars were unsure over extending human rights to children. For instance, the 1948 Universal declaration of Human Rights (UDHR) emphasises that "everyone is entitled to all rights and freedoms set forth in the declaration..." but makes no age qualification to the same. So it is unclear whether it extends to children. However, Article 4 of UDHR has been interpreted as prohibiting exploitation of child labour by interpreting "servitude" to include child labour.

In addition, Articles 23 and 26 of the United Nations Universal Declaration of Human Rights seek to guarantee "just and favourable conditions of work" and the "right to education," both of which are violated constantly and globally through the exercise of the worst forms of child labour.

In 1966 the International Covenant on economic, social and cultural rights (ICESCR) and International Covenant on civil and political rights (ICCPR) took significant preliminary steps towards modifying human rights according to age, by defining childhood as a state requiring special protection, with rights distinct to those of adults. Even so it was not until 1989 that the Convention on Rights of Children (CRC) clearly spelt out the rights of the child while giving them a special status apart from the adults.

Thus, it should not be surprising that early international legal efforts to address child labour tended to be abolitionist in tone and treated as an aspect of labour market regulation. Next, a prioritization approach was adopted where concentration was on the more abusive forms of child labour. So the ILO adopted Convention 182 on the Worst Forms of Child Labour, 1999, aimed at the immediate elimination of intolerable forms of child labour. The convention requires signatories to work with business groups to identify hazardous forms of child labour and introduce time-bound programmes for eliminating them.

Conventions 138 and 182 are recognised as core International Labour Organization (ILO) conventions but unfortunately human rights groups have done much to criticise it. They argue that this artificial division of hazardous and non-hazardous forms of child labour is artificial and made only for the benefit of labour regulations. Child labour in any form is very harmful and exploitative for the children.

Secondly, child labour, as defined by ILO is work done by children under the age of 12; work by children under the age of 15 that prevents school attendance; and work by children under the age of 18 that is hazardous to their physical or mental health. It is an economic activity or work that interferes with the completion of a child's education or that is harmful to children in any way. Such an age based classification is incongruous and is behind time. The right to a childhood cannot be replaced by placing such age barriers which imply at least some work could be done by children at even age 12! Where is the best interest of child seen in such laws?

Fortunately, a human rights approach to child labour was soon adopted by Convention on Rights of the Child (CRC) in 1989. Such rules focus not only on the avoidance of harm to children but as well, on regulation of employment relationship in which working children find themselves and beyond that, on rights of children to education and to participate in decisions that affect their lives, including those related to their employment. This holistic view of child labour as only a part of a child's life is principally what sets human rights approach apart from the labour regulation approach. However, some critique of CRC feel that categorizing child labour as a special category has trivialized their rights and have made them weak and in need of an adult advocate. Conversely, the defenders of CRC argue that it is through this classification that children gain more rights with legally recognized interests which are specific to their stage in life cycle.

The slavery convention, 1926 and Supplementary convention on abolition of slavery, the slave trade, institutions and practices similar to slave trade, 1956 entered into force in 1957 prohibits slavery like practice under Article 1. In recent times Child labour has been read as a slave like practice as it involves economic exploitation. Since children are more vulnerable than adults and are dependent on their parents, it can be assumed that when they are economically exploited by their parents or by their consent, the decree of dependency necessary for work to b qualified as slavery like practice will be attained in most cases.

In the light of ICCPR [Article 8(2)] and Supplementary convention on abolition of slavery, the slave trade, institutions and practices similar to slave trade, 1956, Article 4 of UDHR should be interpretedas prohibiting exploitation of child labour as child labour comes under "servitude". Child labour also comes under the term "forced or compulsory labour" in Article 8(3) of ICCPR. The obligations of state parties under Article 8 are immediate and absolute. Thus state parties have to prevent private parties from violating child labour norms. Article 24, ICCPR obliges the state to protect children from economic exploitation.

Convention on Rights of Child

United Nations Convention on the Rights of the Child is the first legally binding international instrument to incorporate a full range of human rights such as civil, cultural, economic, political and social rights for children. The Convention offers a vision of the child as an individual and as a member of a family and community, with rights and responsibilities appropriate to his or her age and stage of development. By recognizing children's rights in this way, the Convention firmly sets the focus on the whole child.

The Convention under Article 32 speaks of economic exploitation of children by making them perform work that is likely to be hazardous or to interfere with the child's education, or to be harmful to the child's health or physical, mental, spiritual, moral or social development. The Convention spells out a child's right to education, as well as identifying the forms of harm to which children should not be exposed. Other rights given to children include right "to the enjoyment of the highest attainable standard of health" and to abolish traditional practices that are prejudicial to children's health (Article 24), a right "to a standard of living adequate for the child's physical, mental, spiritual, moral and social development"; parents have the main responsibility for this, but governments are required "within their means" to assist parents, as well as to provide material assistance and support in case of need (Article 27) and a right "to rest and leisure, to engage in play and recreational activities appropriate to the age of the child". Article 22 specifies that refugee children have the same rights as all other children.

Article 6 of the convention makes it the obligation of the governments to ensure that children are able to survive and develop "to the maximum extent possible" while Article 11 urges governments to prevent "the illicit transfer and non-return of children abroad". Under Article 19, Governments must take action to protect children against all forms of physical or mental violence, injury, abuse, neglect, maltreatment or exploitation, including sexual abuse and must provide special protection and assistance to children who are deprived of their own family environment under Article 20. Article 35, requires governments to take action to prevent children from being trafficked while articles Articles 36 and 39 requires governments to protect children "against all other forms of exploitation prejudicial to any aspects of the child's welfare" and to help children recover from exploitation, neglect or abuse (particularly their physical and psychological recovery and return and reintegration into the communities they come from).

Two other provisions in the Convention are also vitally important for working children. Article 3 says government agencies and other institutions taking action concerning a child or children must base their decisions on what is in the children's "best interests". Article 12 emphasises that when a child is capable of forming his or her views, these should be given due attention, in accordance with the child's age and maturity.

Other conventions of interest include Optional protocol to the convention on rights of child on sale of children, child prostitution and child pornography and Optional protocol to the convention on rights of child on the involvement of children in armed conflict both adopted in May, 2000.

India and its International Commitments

India has ratified six ILO conventions relating to child labour but have not ratified the core ILO conventions on minimum age for employment (convention 138) and the worst forms of child labour, (convention 182) recognised as the core conventions at the international labour conference which makes it mandatory for the international community to follow certain standards in their crusade against child labour. Nevertheless, India has taken commendable steps to eliminate child labour.

The recent right of children to free and compulsory education Act, 2009 and the preceding 86th amendment exemplifies the same. Furthermore, the passing of Juvenile Justice (Care and Protection) Act, 2006 shows India's commitment to a human rights approach to child labour. The Act emphasises on looking into the best interests of the child and allows for social reintegration of child victims.

In such a scenario India not signing the core labour conventions does not make a difference in the fight against child labour. India is a party to the UN declaration on the Rights of the Child 1959. India is also a signatory to the World Declaration on the Survival, Protection and Development of Children. More, importantly India ratified the Convention on the Rights of the Child on 12 November, 1992.

Other important international initiatives against child labour include the adoption of the first Forced Labour Convention (ILO, No. 29), 1930, Stockholm Declaration and Agenda for Action: States that a crime against a child in one place is a crime anywhere, 1996, establishment of 12 June as the World Day Against Child Labour in 2002 by ILO and the first global economic study on the costs and benefits of elimination of child labour.

Indian Laws on Child Labour

The present regime of laws in India relating to child labour are consistent with the International labour conference resolution of 1979 which calls for combination of prohibitory measures and measures for humanising child labour wherever it cannot be immediately outrun.

In 1986 Child Labour (Prohibition and Regulation) Act was passed, which defines a child as a person who has not completed 14 years of age. The act also states that no child shall be employed or permitted to work in any of the occupations set forth in Part A or in the process set forth in Part B, except in the process of family based work or recognised school based activities. Through a notification dated 27 January, 1999, the schedule has been substantially enlarged to add 6 more occupations and 33 processes to schedule, bringing the total to 13 occupations and 51 processes respectively. The government has amended the civil service (conduct) rules to prohibit employment of a child below 14 years by a government employee. Similar changes in state service rules have also been made.

The framers of the Indian Constitution consciously incorporated relevant provisions in the constitution to secure compulsory primary education as well as labour protection for children. If the provisions of child labour in international conventions such as ILO standards and CRC are compared with Indian standards, it can be said that Indian constitution articulates high standards in some respects The constitution of India, under Articles 23,24, 39 (c) and (f), 45 and 21A guarantees a child free education, and prohibits trafficking and employment of children in factories etc. The articles also protect children against exploitation and abuse. Equality provisions in the constitution authorises affirmative action policies on behalf of the child.

The National Child Labour, Policy (1987) set up national child labour projects in areas with high concentration of child labour in hazardous industries or occupations, to ensure that children are rescued from work and sent to bridge schools which facilitate mainstreaming. It is now recognised that every child out of school is a potential child labour and most programmes working against child labour tries to ensure that every child gets an education and that children do not work in situations where they are exploited and deprived of a future. Similarly, there are other programmes like National Authority for Elimination of

Child Labour, 1994 (NAECL) and National Resource Centre on Child Labour, 1993 (NRCCL). Recently, government of India notified domestic child labour, and child labour in dhabas, hotels, eateries, spas and places of entertainment as hazardous under the Child Labour (Prohibition and Regulation) Act, 1986, effective from 10-10-2006.

National human rights commission has played an important role in taking up cases, of worst forms of child labour like bonded labour. In 1991 in a silk weaving village of Karnataka called Magdi it held an open hearing which greatly sensitised the industry and civil societies. It also gave rise to new NCLP programmes.

Judicial Reflections

Judiciary in India has taken a proactive stand in eradicating child labour. In the case of M.C. Mehta v. State of Tamil Nadu and Ors., this Court considered the causes for failure to implement the constitutional mandate *vis-a-vis* child labour. It was held that the State Government should see that adult member of family of child labour gets a job. The labour inspector shall have to see that working hours of child are not more than four to six hours a day and it receives education at least for two hours each day. The entire cost of education was to be borne by employer. The same was reiterated in Bandhua Mukti Morchav. UOI and directions were given to the Government to convene meeting of concerned ministers of State for purpose of formulating policies for elimination of employment of children below 14 years and for providing necessary education, nutrition and medical facilities. It was observed in both the case that it is through education that the vicious cycle of poverty and child labour can be broken. Further, well-planned, poverty-focussed alleviation, development and imposition of trade actions in employment of the children must be undertaken. Total banishment of employment may drive the children and mass them up into destitution and other mischievous environment, making them vagrant, hard criminals and prone to social risks etc. Immediate ban of child labour would be both unrealistic and counter-productive. Ban of employment of children must begin from most hazardous and intolerable activities like slavery, bonded labour, trafficking, prostitution, pornography and dangerous forms of labour and the like.

Also, in case of PUCL v. UOI and Ors. children below 15 years forced to work as bonded labour was held to be violative of Article 21 and hence the children were to be compensated. The court further observed that such a claim in public law for compensation for contravention of human rights and fundamental freedoms, the protection of which is guaranteed in the Constitution, is an acknowledged remedy for enforcement and protection of such rights.

However, Human rights experts criticise the scheme of payment of compensation envisage in Child labour act and further adopted by the Judiciary with gusto. They say that monetary compensation is like washing away ones conscious which still believes that if a child labour is sent to school he must be compensated for the amount which he might have got if he had worked instead. This only confuses the already divided opinion of the society today which still thinks that poor and needy children are better off working.

India has done well in enacting suitable legislations and policies to combat child labour. Nonetheless, its implementation at grass root level is very much lacking. The child labour laws today are like a scarecrow which does not eliminate child labour but only shifts it geographically to other places, to other occupations like agriculture which may be less paying or it might be still continued clandestinely. The lack of a specialised enforcement officer leads to lesser attention being given to child labour legislations. Furthermore, many of the child labour programmes remain poorly funded.

Child Labours as Social Evil

Child labour is a complex problem which cannot be eliminated without first attacking it at the roots. Thus, poverty, unemployment, lack of social security schemes, illiteracy and the attitude of society need to be tackled first before any progress can be made. A starting point can be to treat Child labour as a human rights problem and discouraging its manifestation in any form. If the society as such sees child labour as a social malaise, we will be much closer at achieving success. Lastly, there is a lot of debate over the age from which child labour should be banned. The ILO conventions do not give a definite age, 14 years seems to be the general understanding but CRC defines a child to be below 18 years. Right to education is for children below 14 years and Child labour is prohibited till age of 14 years. This brings the question as to whether children of age 14-18 years are to be denied basic human rights and are to be left vulnerable.

'How sad, many girls missing from our country are found buried in some graveyard....

India is growing dynamically in every fields. Today, the boom in economy, innovative technologies and "improved infrastructure has become nation's pride. The country has witnessed advancements in all fields but bias against a girl child is still prevailing in the country.

This social evil is deep rooted in Indian ethos and the most shocking fact is that the innovative and hard high end technologies are brutally killing the Indian girl child. Innovative techniques, like biopsy, ultrasound, scan tests and amniocentesis, devised to detect genetic abnormalities, are highly misused by number of families to detect gender of the unborn child. These clinical tests are highly contributing to the rise in genocide of the unborn girl child.

In today's day and age most couples prefer the process known as a planned pregnancy, because of various factors; prime amongst them being the financial well being to support the birth and nurturing of a child. In such cases, the first prenatal visit actually happens prior to actual pregnancy, to see whether one is ready to go off the contraception pills and conceive a baby. However, in maximum conceptions, one is unaware of the pregnancy until actual realization dawns after one skips the first menstrual cycle. Normally doctors except ladies to pay their first visit anywhere between the sixth and twelfth week after conception.

Amniocentesis started in India in 1974 to detect fetal abnormalities. These tests were used to detect gender for the first time in 1979 in Amritsar, Punjab. Later the test was stopped by the Indian Council of Medical Research but it was too late. The benefits of these tests were leaked out and people started using it as an instrument for killing an innocent and unborn girl child. Many of the traditional women organizations also took up cudgels to stop this illegal practice but all failed and with the passage of time these tests became a major contributor to bias against a girl child.

Female feticide and infanticide is not the only issues with a girl child in India. At every stage of life she is discriminated and neglected for basic nutrition, education and living standard. When she was in the womb, she was forced to miss the moment when she was supposed to enter the world. At the time of birth her relatives pulled her back and wrung her neck. After killing her she was thrown into a trash can.

During childhood, her brother was loaded with new shoes, dresses and books to learn while she was gifted a broom, a wiper and lots of tears. In her teenage, she missed tasty delicious food to eat and got only the crumbs. During her college days, she was forced to get married, a stage where illiteracy, lack of education resulted in high fertility rate, aggravating the condition of females in the country. Again if this female gives birth to a girl child, the journey begins once again. She missed all roses of life and was finally fitted to a graveyard. That's where she got peace of mind.

Conclusion

The nation of mothers still follows a culture where people idolizes son and mourns daughters. UN figures out that about 750,000 girls are aborted every year in India. Abortion rates are increasing in almost 80% of the India states, mainly Punjab and Haryana. These two states have the highest number of abortions every year. If the practice continues, then no longer a day will come when Mother India will have no mothers, potentially, no life.

We all are proud citizens of India. The need of hour is to realize our responsibilities and give a halt to this evil crime. What can we do to curb the brutal and undesirable practice of mass killing girls? A determined drive can initiate a spark to light the lamp and show the world that we all are part of the great Mother India.

Human Rights Management after Globalization **Pages 123-129**
Edited by: Dr. Rabi Narayana Misra
ISBN: 978-93-88854-05-4
Edition: 2019
Published by: Discovery Publishing House Pvt. Ltd., New Delhi (India)

Chapter 12

Role of Madduri Annapurnayya in Andhra Socialist Movement

[1]Dr. B. Raja Rao

Madduri Annapurnayya was born on 20-03-1899 to Madduri Jayaramayya & Rajamma at Komaragiri, near Pithapuram in the present East Godavari District of Andhra Pradesh. His grandfather Kodanda Rama Dikshitulu was a wealthy person. He was well known for his charity.

He studied his primary Education at Pithapuram, Peddapuram & Tuni which are nearer to his place. After schooling career he joined at Pithapuram Raja's Collegiate, High School, Kakinada in 1911, as a student of III form. During this time he had the opportunity to meet with a great patriot and freedom fighter-**Alluri Sitarama Raju,** who was his classmate. After a few days he became a close associate **of Alluri Sitarama Raju.** Even in those days, Annapurnayya had love of freedom, noble ideas and respect for values. Pithapuram Raja's College is one of the premier Institutions of Higher Education in Coastal Andhra. In those days Brahmarshi Raghupati Venktaratnam Naidu, Principal of P.R. College Kandukuri Veeresalingam Panthulu of Rajahmundry were eminent educationists and social reforms. They exercised great influence on the minds of young man and women especially on the college students. The students of P.R. College like Madduri Annapurnayya, Madduri Kodanda Rama Dikshitulu, (Elder brother of Annapurnayya) and Alluri Sitarama Raju etc., had profound influence of their teachers especially, their principal Brahmarshi Raghupati Venktaratnam.

[1] Principal, Government Degree College Seethanagaram, East Godavari, Andhra Pradesh

So far as research has been undertaken on National events in connection with the leaders. We know that in each and every national event of the freedom struggle, the local leaders played an important role like Madduri Annapurnayya in Costal Andhra area popularly known as Andhra Netaji.

Madduri Annapurnayya was the sole worker in popularizing the congress socialist movement in Andhra Pradesh. His long stay in various jails gave an opportunity to meet different ideological leaders and patriots. Later on it proved to be an invaluable source of political education which was the turning point towards socialism. During his jail life he studied Socialist literature, and Marxism. He knew many things about soviet Russia. He happened to meet a few Marxists in different jails. During this time he digested the essence of socialism.

Jayaprakash Narayan was the secretary of all India Congress Socialist Party; when he toured Andhra Region, Madduri accompanied him. Abolition of the Zamindari system and feudalism were the main slogans of the Propaganda of Madduri, during his accompanying with Jayaprakash Narayana. He demanded proprietary rights for the farmers who actually tilled the land.

Birth of Andhra Congress Socialist Forum

In 1934 during the freedom movement, Jayaprakash Narayana attended the political meeting held at Visakhapatnam Andhra Socialist leaders like Kambhampati Satyanarayana, Jonnalagadde Ramalingayya, Chundi Jagannadham, Gopala Reddy etc., attended the meeting. Tenneti Viswanadham was elected its president and Madduri Annapurnayya was elected the chief Secretary of Congress Socialist Forum. Gowthu Latchanna, Alluri Satyanarayana, Putchalapalli Sundara Ramayya became the Executive members of the Forum. So it is a fact that the Andhra Congress Socialist Forum was formed in 1934, in the above meeting with the invaluable services of Madduri Annapurnayya.

The Golden Jubilee celebrations of the AICC were held at Rajahmundry in 1935. So many leaders were invited to the function. Annapurnayya played a prominent role in that celebrations. At the same time his wife was severely suffering from Typhoid fever. He loved her most still he paid more interest in the successful completion of these Golden Jubilee celebrations of the All India Congress Committee.

The second Andhra Socialist Congress Party meeting was held at Rajahmundry on 26th & 27th of September, 1936. Madduri Annapurnayya was elected secretary and Krovvidi Lingaraju and Putchalapalli Sundearayya became the Joint Secretaries of the conference from 1936 onwards Annapurnayya one of the close associates of Lokmanya Jayaprakash Narayana. Since 1936, he was also a member of AICC. From 1936 to 6th April 1940 he arranged and conducted many activities which were helpful to the common man in the society.

He presided over the political meeting at Lankalakoderu in the west Godavari on 30th Jan., 1939, which was inaugurated by Smt. Kamaladevi Chatopadhya. He advised the youth specially to know the facts and to think for a while about dare responsibilities in the making of Indian socialism. Annapurnayya had a great respect towards Lenin. He called J.P. the Lenin of India, Mahidhara jaganmohan Rao, translated J.P.'s Book, "Why Socialism" into Telugu with the title of "Socialism Enduku" with the inspiration of Madduri Annapurnayya, who wrote "Forework" to the book.

Annapurnayya started Navasakti paper on 15-12-1937 for the propagation of his socialistic ideas. It became the backbone of the socialist party through which he brought his socialistic ideas to the doorsteps of the common people. Subsequently the Navasakthi was transformed into 'Prajasakthi' a daily, published by the communists.

In March 1937 as the Chief Secretary of the Andhra Congress Socialist Party, Annapurnayya published the **code and conduct** of the socialist party members. They are as followed;

1. Only members of the Congress are eligible to be members of the, Congress Socialist Party.

2. Members should accept the doctrines of Karl Marks and study the science of class convict and relevant duties.

3. Aims and objectives of the All India Congress Socialist Party are as follows:

1. Administrative power should be vested in the hands of the producers and the ordinary people.
2. The economic life of the country should be regulated and developed by the Government in a systematic manner.
3. The instruments of production, distribution etc., should be transferred to the society gradually and in a phased programme.
4. Co-operative Credit Societies should be started.
5. Transactions with foreign countries should be conducted by the Government.
6. State and Zamindaries should be abolished without any compensation.
7. Land should be distributed among the tillers of the soil.
8. Co-operative forming should be encouraged.
9. The debts of workers and farmers should be cancelled.
10. Right to work should be recognized or the Government should accept the responsibility to look after the people.
11. Work awarding to capacity and remuneration according to need concept should be attached.
12. Everyone, who attains the age of majority, should have voting rights.
13. Government should be above caste, community etc.
14. Public Debt of India need not be honored.

He united the workers of the Alluminium business and press workers of Rajahmundry when there was difference among them. Later on he became the honorary president of the above mentioned unions and served for their stability and socio-economic developments.

Nava Sakthi - Telugu Weekly

Navashakthi was started and published on 15-12-1937 with a photo of Karl Marx on the title page. The Slogan "Workers and Farmers to unite" was on the front page. It was the first weekly or the paper in Andhra on behalf of the Communists. Annapurnayya explained the principal objectives in the paper in the following words: "This paper accepts the socialist system. It strengthens the Congress Freedom Struggle and assists in fearing the doctrine of imperialism to shreds." He started this paper of the Congress Socialist party in Andhra Subsequently the Navashakthi transformed into "Prajashathi" a daily published by the communists.

Kothapatnam Camp

Prof. Ranga was the president and Annapurnayya was the secretary of the Andhra Province Congress Socialist Party.

On may 1st, 1937 the Congress Socialist Party organized a training CAMP AT Kothapatnam. The main aim and objectives of the camp was to create new political outlook and Philosophy in their minds. Kothapatnam is 15 km away from Ongole town. The camp was attended by 170 volunteers. The main participants were Putchalapalli Sundarayya, Kolla Venkaiah, Makkineni Basavapunnaiah, Jonnalagadda Ramalingaiah, Pidathala Rangareddy etc. Later on they became prominent leaders. The camp was held for 20 days from 1st May, 1937 to 20th May, 1937.

The resource persons were Indulal Yagnik, Zahill Hazzra Begum, Swamy Sahajananda Saraswathi, Acharya Ranga, Jayprakash Narayan, Achutpatwardhan, Batliwada & CP Alongo etc. Annnapragadha Kameswara Rao and Madduri Annapurnayya, Alluri Satyanarayana Raju, Neti Chalapathi and Sagi Vijayaramaraju shouldered the responsibility of running the training camp.

The training camp was a great success. So naturally the Govt. banned the camp and in May, 1937 the then Collector of Guntur District raided the camp with two vans of police men and lathy charged and inmates of the camp. Annapurnayya and Annapragada and others were injured.

Manthenavaripalem Camp

On 4th May, 1938 Annapragda Kameswara Rao arranged another training camp at Manthevaripalem in Guntur

District. Fortunately this camp was not banned by the Govt. Annapurnayya delivered lectures on Indian national congress and socialism. Prominent leaders like Madabhusha Venkatachary, Chandra Rajeswara Rao, C.V.K. Rao, Kambhapati Satyanarayana, P.V. Sivayya Jonnalagadda Rama Lingaiah, S.A. Donge and P.C. Joshi and others visited the camp as observers. The sole idea of the camp was to motivate the youth towards Indian freedom movement with selfless activities through socialism. This camp was started on 4-5-1938 which continued for one month.

He tried his level best to solve the following issues as his own. They are as follows:

1. Latlhy charge on socialists in Vijayawada.
2. Dictatorial activities of police on the poor people at Muramanda.
3. The natural disaster or a sad even of the Koya Farmers of Vandegudem and Butchayyapeta in 1947.
4. The incidents occurred at Almanda village near srungavarapukota between Ryots and Revenue officers and also the issue aroused at Kalipatnam etc., were taken by him. His commitment and courage impressed Jaya Prakash Narayana much. Both of them were Gandhians at the initial stage and faithfully followed him. They were skilled orators. Later on they became Marxists. Out of their experiences, they realized and turned into spiritual life at the last stage.

Findings

The Andhra Congress socialist movement awakened the youth to think themselves about the nation and the national issues those who later on played a vital role in the freedom struggle and in the remaking of the nation through the weekly Telugu paper Navashakthi. Medduri demanded proprietary rights for the farmers who actually tilled the land. The purpose of the starting of the Navashakti was to motivate the people into activity when they were leading a passive and idle life. He wanted to instill patriotism and sacrifice in them and makes them agents of future democratic or self-Government.

REFERENCES

1. Dr. Raja Rao, B. Sitanagara Sevasrama Charitra (1924-89). Published by B. Padmavathi, Sitanagaram.
2. Rajagopala Rao C. V., Gowtami Satyagraha Asharaman, Sitanagaram, Published by Vishalandra Publishing House, Hyderabad.
3. Gangadhara Rama Rao, Tulasi. Swatantriya Samidhulu, published by Tulasi Gangadhara Rama Rao, Rajahmundry.
4. Prof. Chalapathi Rao, LV. Veteran Freedom Fighter, Eminent Journalist Madduri Annapurnayya Published by Madduri Annapurnayya, Birth Centinary Celebrations Committee, 1 73, Lalithanagar, Hyderabad.
5. Andhra Pradesh District Gazetters, E.G.D.
6. Kesava Narayana B. Political and Social Factors in Andhra, Nevodaya Publisher, Vijayawada, 1976.

Human Rights Management after Globalization **Pages 130-141**
Edited by: Dr. Rabi Narayana Misra
ISBN: 978-93-88854-05-4
Edition: 2019
Published by: Discovery Publishing House Pvt. Ltd., New Delhi (India)

Chapter 13
Human Rights after Globalization in India

[1]Dr. G. Chandrayya
[2]Dr. Rookesh K. Misra

Introduction

The world's inequalities are constantly growing : millions of people continue to suffer from forced evictions, inadequate access to education and basic health treatment and appalling working conditions. Economic actors, especially multinational corporations, have acquired increased power in the past decades. Liberalisation of trade and investment flows, protection granted to foreign investors, the high degree of dependency between the world's economies but also foreign debt and policies of international financial institutions have restrained the ability of States to uphold their human rights obligations. Human rights defenders and those participating in protests denouncing corporate abuse are being increasingly targeted. Communities struggle to obtain justice for violations of economic, social and cultural rights, even more so when involving multinational companies that operate across national borders.

FIDH advocates for the full recognition and justiciability of economic, social and cultural rights and campaigns for the ratification of the Optional Protocol to the International Covenant on Economic, Social and Cultural Rights. Together with its member organisations, FIDH works with communities throughout the world to ensure corporate accountability and improve victims' access to justice through documentation, advocacy and litigation. FIDH calls on States to take their

1 Asst. Prof., Government Degree College, Ravulapalem, Andhra Pradesh.
2 H.R. Manager, New Delhi.

human rights obligations into account when they negotiate trade and investment agreements with third countries and promotes respect for human rights and the environment in investment.

Meaning of Globalisation

Globalisation is a process of interaction and integration among the people, companies and governments of different nations, a process driven by international trade and investment and aided by information technology. This process has effects on the environment, on culture, on political systems, on economic development and prosperity and on human physical well-being in societies around the world.

Social workers approach globalisation from a human rights perspective as set out in the IFSW/IASSW international Ethical Statement. Social workers recognise the benefits and disadvantages of globalization for the most vulnerable people in the world. Our professional perspective focuses especially on how the economic and environmental consequences affect social relationships and individual opportunity.

Globalization can seem a remote process, related only to the economic and commercial world. So how would greater attention to human rights change any of these realities? First, the human rights framework adds to development policy the notion that education, food, adequate housing and health care are rights, not merely needs.

This implies that the poor should not simply benefit from more resources, but must have legal and political space to claim their rights and take part in decision-making. It implies that government policies should ensure access to justice, protect against discrimination, and fulfill economic and social rights. In designing social safety nets, and poverty reduction strategies, their policies must respect the right to an adequate standard of living, including food, housing, health protection, education and social security.

An example of how globalization has affected people's basic rights and resulted in people becoming displaced from their homes centers on the availability of water. 900 million people in the world do not have access to clean water. 2.5 billion people have no safe way to dispose of human waste—many defecate in open fields or near the same rivers they drink from. Dirty water and lack of a toilet and proper hygiene kill 3.3 million people around the world annually, most of them children under age five. Some of the reasons for water becoming such a critical issue are the building of dams, climate change and unequal investment in the infrastructure of basic services.

It often falls to women and children to carry water in some of the most critical areas of the world. One of the issues for charities who have helped communities build wells and other methods of access to water is that when the NGO has moved out the community the infrastructure has not been there in the community to sustain the water project, there may be an issue of trust with each other about finding the few dollars to fund a spare part or having the local necessary skills to make the repair. This aspect of helping groups and communities work together is very much part of using social work skills to make sure that people can achieve change in their lives, in this case making sure that water, needed for living is readily available.

Would globalization enhance the implementation of human rights as stated in the Universal Declaration of Human Rights (1948) and the subsequent United Nations agreements, particularly the covenant on Civil and Political Rights (1966), the covenant on Economic, Social and Cultural Rights (1966) and the declaration on the Right to Development (1986)?

Attempting an answer to this question is not an easy task, mainly because of the different and contradictory connotations of the term globalization.

If globalization is conceived as turning the whole world into one global village in which all peoples are increasingly inter-connected and all the fences or barriers are removed, so that the world witnesses a new state of fast and free flow of people, capital, goods and ideas then the world would be witnessing unprecedented enjoyment of human rights every where because globalization is bringing prosperity to all the corners of the globe together with the spread of the highly cherished values of democracy, freedom and justice (1).

On the other hand if globalization is conceived as turning the world into a global market for goods and service dominated and steered by the powerful gigantic transnational corporations and governed by the rule of profit then all the human rights of the people in the world, particularly in the south would be seriously threatened (2).

Literature on globalization, in general, by both the so called advocates and opponents of globalization is abundant. However, the critics of globalization lay much more emphasis on its impact on human rights, particularly of the poor people and of the developing countries. Their analysis and conclusions are usually supported by facts and figures drawn from international reports and statistics to prove that human rights have been adversely affected by globalization. They usually relate one or the other aspect of human rights to one or the other aspect of globalization, such as relating poverty in developing countries to debt or relating unemployment to privatization, or relating health deterioration to the monopoly of medicine patents. Or they enumerate the aspects of deteriorations in human rights, such as impoverishment and lowering standards of living, increasing inequality discrimination, deprivation of satisfaction of basic needs such as food clean water and housing, illiteracy etc., and explain these facts by globalization in general through making comparisons between the state before globalization (usually before the 1990s) and after it, such as stating that "progress in reducing infant mortality was considerably slower during the period of globalization (1990-1998) than over the previous two decades."

The advocates of globalization do not deny the fact that in some regions basic human rights are not respected during the past decade but they explain this by the resistance of some countries and peoples to globalization and they claim that globalization must have winners and losers. The losers resistance to globalization is attributed to their state of stagnation and rigidity or to their traditional culture or even to the nature of their religions which is anti-democratic and anti-modernization (3).

So both advocates and critics of globalization agree on the fact that human rights are in some way or the other adversely affected by globalization particularly in the south, but they differ in their explanation of this fact and hence in their prescription for the remedies. While the advocates prescribe more absorption of peoples and countries in the global system, the critics of globalization prescribe opposition and resistance of the hegemony of the transnational corporations and the injustice inherent in the globalization process. Who is right ? to answer this question we need, as I think, to examine the underlying basic assumptions of both the human rights agreements and the globalization agreements, particularly the economic, which I believe are contradictory as far as human rights are concerned.

Contradictory Basic Assumptions of Human Rights and Globalization

The underlying basic assumption upon which all UN human rights agreements were based was governments' responsibility while globalization basic underlying assumption has been from the very beginning government relief from any responsibility regarding human rights.

All human rights agreements were discussed, negotiated and signed by governments and all the declarations were addressed to governments who were held responsible for either their implementation or violations. Governments were asked to take whatever political, economic, social, cultural and legislative measures to enhance the implementation of human rights in their countries. All human rights annual reports on the state of human rights in countries of the world published by UN, human rights societies or some countries such as USA held government responsible for violations of human rights. governments were assumed to be policy and decision-makers for all economic, political and social domains in their countries.

Since the Universal declaration of Human rights in 1948 many countries of the world, whether in the north or the south succeed in enhancing the implementation of human rights, particularly in the economic, social and cultural domains simply through policies of subsidizing food, housing and services such as health care, transportation, sanitation, culture and education. Many countries, particularly in the south made considerable achievements in the field of the right to work simply by taking decisions to protect local industries from competition and thus creating job opportunities for their population.

On the contrary globalization agreements require governments to abide by the global market mechanisms and to follow the advices (instructions) of the international agencies such as WTO, IMF and the World Bank.

So governments have to be decision-takers rather than decision-makers particularly in the economic domain and they have to make all necessary adjustments and restructuralisations in their societal systems. They have to issue new laws in every sphere to facilitate the operations of the free market mechanism and to cancel any existing laws which hamper this operation. They may even have to change articles in their constitutions, such as those related to public and private sectors. Many of those changed laws are related to human rights particularly the economic, social and cultural rights. The most important of these changes are related to taxation, worker-employer relations, owner-renter relations, government subsidization of basic needs goods such as food, water and housing and services such as education, health, transportation, and even mass communication and cultural services (such as telephones, newspapers, theatres, books and television). Every thing has to be dealt with as a market commodity judged by its economic value rather than its social value.

The adoption of the wide open door policy by governments requires issuing laws which impedes another fundamental human right declared by UN, that is the right to development. Laws allowing the free flow of capital and goods with almost no restrictions on imports through tariffs adversely affect local developmental projects.

So governments find themselves in a very paradoxical situation. If they try to abide by UN human rights agreements which they signed they would be violating the globalizations agreements, which they also signed! and they would be criticized or even penalized for this violation (by cutting the aids offered to them by international institutions), and if they try to abide by globalization agreements they would be necessarily violating the human rights agreements and would be criticized for that in the human right reports and the UN statistics on human development would show them lagging behind in indices of human development.

How Governments Face the Contradiction?

Governments, particularly of the developing countries, have been persuaded and pressured to sacrifice human rights for the sake of globalization.

Violations of human rights agreements, particularly those of economic, social and cultural rights are not met by practical punishments or deterrence measures. The reactions of both international organizations and local human rights groups do not exceed criticism, condemnation or demonstrations at most. On the contrary violations of economic rules of globalization and agreements are met with very severe practical measures such as economic boycotting and cutting of aids.

Many authors provide evidence on the adverse effects of governments adoption of globalization economic agreements on basic human rights due to the reduced overall government spending on services and satisfaction of basic human needs and the increasing tendencies towards privatization of these services.

Vandana Shiva states that "during 1979-81 and 1992-1993, calorie intake declined by three per cent in Mexico, 4.1 per cent in Argentina, 10.9 per cent in Kenya, 10.0 per cent in Tanzania, 9.9 percent in Ethiopia. In India, the per capita cereal consumption declined by 12.2 for rural areas and 5.4 per cent in urban areas. "She explains these figures by saying that countries cannot ensure that the hungry are fed because this involves laws, policies and financial commitments which are "protectionist".

She also offers evidence on the impact of globalization agreements on the right to health: "Under the trade Related Intellectual Property agreement of the World Trade Organization, countries have to implement patent laws granting exclusive, monopolistic rights to the pharmaceutical and biotech industry. This prevents countries from producing low cost generic drugs. Patented HIV/AIDS medicine costs $15,000, while generic drugs made by India and Brazil cost $250-300 for one years treatment. Patents are, therefore robbing AIDS victims of their rights".

Diana Smith shows how the policies associated with globalization affected primary health care services. She states that : "introducing the market mechanism into the provision of health care obviously makes services less available to the poor. The privatization of health and hospital services also makes the poor suffer as services become more oriented towards those who can pay. In addition, essential drug policies, which aim to make necessary pharmaceuticals available to all at an affordable price, are threatened by increasingly liberal policies towards pharmaceutical companies. Finally, increasing unemployment and poverty add to the nations health problems by creating extra demands on reduced government services." (5)

The authors of Global Issues state that "the lives of 1.7 million children will be needlessly lost this year (2002) because world governments have failed to reduce poverty levels" and "Progress in life expectancy was also reduced for 4 out of 5 groups of countries, with the exception of the highest group (life expectancy 69-76 years), also "progress in reducing infant mortality was also considerably slower during the last two decades than over the previous decades". (6)

T. Rajamoorthy states that "globalization resulted in the violation of the fundamental right to work. In their drive for profits, companies, in particular TNCs, have been restructuring their operations on a global scale. The result has been massive unemployment. In 1995, the ILO announced that one third of the world's willing to work population was either unemployed or underemployed .... the goal of full employment, which was one of the pillars of the social consensus that prevailed after the Second World War, has been jettisoned by nearly all governments .... Globalization has also engendered or accentuated the process of the casualization and informalization of labour". He mentions that only 8 per cent of the labour force in India is in the formal economy while 90 per cent work in the informal economy with no legal protection or security and are subject to ruthless exploitation. Many companies including TNCs got rid of their unionized labour force and moved their operations to law wage and depressed areas to avail themselves of the large supply of unorganized and unprotected, mainly female labour. (7)

Mathews George Chunakara describes the state of workers in developing countries after globalization as a race to the bottom and the bottom means slave like conditions. He explains this by the search of transnational companies for cheap labour in order to maximize their profits, so the governments of developing countries compete for the investors by providing cheaper labour. (8)

The right to education has been also adversely affected by the privatization policies and the turning of education into a profit generating enterprises in the developing countries. Due to the reduced governmental expenditure on education the quality of public free education has suffered a lot. Investors established educational institutes covering all the range from kinder gardens to universities offering better but much more expensive quality of education for the elites and motivated mainly by profit. However most developing countries still suffer a high rate of illiteracy and graduates of the governmental low quality educational institutions are not well prepared for the labour market so they suffer unemployment.

Danilo Turk showed that the globalization agreements and policies had its adverse effects on the right to work, the right to food, the right to health, the right to education and the right to development. (9)

There is almost a consensus over the fact that the human rights are much more adversely affected by globalization in the south or the so called developing countries. One of those adversely affected fundamental rights is the right to development. "When countries loose their right to regulate the entry, behaviour and operations of foreign investment in the interests of their own people, it is not difficult to appreciate why it is bound to result in an impairment of the right to development. (10)

Consequences of Violations of Human Rights

No doubt that the widespread violations of human rights is related to the widening gap between the rich and the poor, both on the global and on the local levels. International Statistics prove this fact. (11) It shows that:

- Half the world - nearly three billion people - live on less than two dollars a day.
- The wealthiest nation on earth has the widest gap between rich and poor of any industrialized nation.
- The top fifth of the world's people in the richest countries enjoy 82% of the expanding export trade and 68% of foreign direct investment - while the bottom fifth, barely more than 1%.
- In 1960, the 20% of the worlds people in the richest countries had 30 times the income of the poorest 20% — in 1997, 74 times as much.
- A few hundred millionaires now own as much wealth as the world's poorest 2.5 billon people.
- The combined wealth of the world's 200 richest people hit $ 1 trillion in 1999; the combined incomes of the 582 million people living in the 43 Beast developed countries is $ 146 billion.
- This leads to an increasing feelings of deprivation and injustice among the populations of the different countries of the world which is enhanced by the rapid and unprecedented advance in communication and information technologies, which really turned the

world in this respect into a global village. The deprived are exposed daily, if not every minute to images and evidences of the huge gap in standards of living between the rich and the poor.

Some consequences of this deprivations of human rights are social and political unrest and even violence and counter violence . It also leads to an increasing resort to suppression and to chaos. Paradoxically the expenditure on suppressing protest and violence may be equal to or even exceeds the ought to be expenditure on implementing economic, social and cultural human rights for all the peoples of the world. What matters more is the loss of human lives and the loss of constructive contributions which all the deprived could have offered to the economic, social, scientific and cultural advancement of humanity if they were granted their basic human rights. Racism, prejudices, and discrimination are negatively associated with justice and implementation of human rights.

There is enough evidence that the world wealth is, in general, rapidly increasing due to the advance in science and technology and that it is more than enough to satisfy the needs of all the dwellers of the globe. What is needed is the globalization of human rights and prosperity, but how ?

Globalization and the Human Rights Approach

Mary Robinson stressed the fact that "A key characteristic of economic globalization is that the actors involved are not only states, but private power in the form of multinational or transnational corporations. It is now the case that more than half of the top economies in the world are corporations not states, and international investment is increasingly private ." She states that there is a trend towards holding companies accountable through legal rules for the human rights and environmental impact of their policies, she says that corporations should ensure that they uphold and respect human rights as reflected in the Universal Declarations of Human Rights and are not themselves complicit in human rights abuses.

But if we acknowledge that transnational corporations are much powerful than the states, particularly those of the dependant developing countries then who would issue those badly needed legal rules and who would implement them ? Transnational corporations which are steering the economic globalization are not at all directed by ethical or humanitarian principles. The maximization of profit is the major if not the only driving force for all their activities.

To be logical I tend to think like this : if economic corporations became transnational and that much powerful what is needed is a powerful transnational government based on real democracy for all the countries and citizens of the world. A government which is capable of issuing and implementing global rules aimed at realization of the maximum use of all humankind achievements for the sake of all the dwellers of our globe. A government which is capable of making economy in the service of man instead of making man a victim and a slave for the market economy.

REFERENCES

1. Thomas L. Friedman : The lexus and the Olive Tree : Understanding Globalization, Cairo : International Publishers, 1999.
2. Anthony Giddens : "Globalization", BBC Reith Lectures. (http://www.Ise. ac.uk/Giddens __99/week! htm)
3. Leslie Sklair, Globalization-Capitalism and its Alternatives, Oxford University Press, 2002.
4. Gray C. Hufbaur, Globalization Facts and Consequences Institute for International Economics, 2001. http://www. üe. com/papers/ hufbaur1000.htm)
5. Paul L. S.J., Education for Globalization, America Press, 2002 http://www. americapress. org/articles/locatelli. htm
6. Vandana Shiva, Violence of Globalization, The Hindu (New Delhi, India) March 25, 2001.
   http://www.zmag.org/crises CurEvts/shivaglob.htm
7. Theodore Levitt, The Globalization of Markets "Harvard Business Review 61 (3) (May-June): 92-102.

Human Rights Management after Globalization **Pages 142-145**
Edited by: Dr. Rabi Narayana Misra
ISBN: 978-93-88854-05-4
Edition: 2019
Published by: Discovery Publishing House Pvt. Ltd., New Delhi (India)

Chapter 14

Economic Development and Human Rights

[1]S. Venugopal

Introduction

Now-a-days, violation of 'Human rights' in various form seems to be very common in every corner of the world, especially in the context of increasing economic activities under Globalization. India is not an exception to such violation as more number of incidents of violating human rights are registered everywhere in the country. Now the slogan of 'Protecting Human Rights' is echoed from all quarters of the world. It is the time for every citizen, society and Government to reconcile the safe guards of human rights. The presentation of this seminar paper has two-fold objectives:

1. To reiterate the concept of 'Universal declaration of human rights'.
2. To deal with issues related to economic development and human rights.

Universal Declaration of Human Rights

Since World War-II, there has been an increasing concern throughout the world to secure human rights for all. As an expression of this, the United Nations Charter reaffirmed 'faith in fundamental human rights'. The universal declaration of human rights, approved by the U.N. General Assembly on 10th December, 1948, inaugurated a new understanding of human rights in the contemporary era. It states that recognition of the inherent dignity and of the equal rights of all members of

[1] M.A. M.Phil, Dept. of Economics, Govt. Degree College Ravulapalem, E.G. Distt.

human family is the foundation of freedom, justice and peace in the world. The following are the universal declaration of human rights:

1. International convention of Economics, Social and Cultural rights.
2. Declaration on the right to development.
3. Convention against discrimination in Education.
4. Convention on the elimination of all forms of discrimination against women.
5. Convention on abolition of forced labour.
6. Convention on right to organize and collective bargaining.
7. Universal declaration on the eradication of hunger and malnutrition.
8. Convention on equal remuneration for men and women workers of equal value.
9. Convention on Employment policy.
10. Declaration on the use of Scientific and technological progress in the interest of peace and for the benefit of mankind.
11. Convention on the right of child.

It proclaims that 'all human beings are born free and equal in dignity and rights'. It deals not only with civil and political rights but also with economic, social and cultural rights such as the right to work, right to choose one's work freely, right to earn equal pay for equal work, right to education etc.

Everyone in this world is entitled to all the rights and freedoms set forth in the declaration, without distinction of any kind. Every citizen, society and state shall strive to promote respect for these rights and freedom and secure their effective implementation.

Economic Development and Human Rights

India is a fast growing economy that have been experienced rapid economic growth. Despite this remarkable growth, Human Rights abuses still play a significant role in many parts of the country. Economic development has had a strong impact, worsening livelihoods of the people and the conditions of the lands in many parts of the country. Thanks to establishment of many industrial projects in resource-rich parts of the country, people are compelled to leave their land without adequate compensation.

No doubt projects have been major vehicles of development. But a project constitutes a deliberate, planned intervention by the outside agencies into the lives of the people. Most projects are intended to change the behaviour of target people by altering their social and physical environments. Now some of the development projects generate some risks and harms to some categories of project-affected people. Projects to construct large scale dams are notorious producers of large number of victims. Construction of dams produce significant human displacement including hundreds of communities of tribal and forest people who held their ancestral lands. The process of getting compensation become extraordinarily difficult to illiterate people as it is very difficult to them to prove their land holding rights and losses. It is often argued that organizations that deal with economic development should avoid Human Rights issues because these two topics are distinct.

Despite the benefits of economic development, the country is experiencing other grave Human Rights concerns that are damaging India's economic social and cultural rights. It is true that millions of people have to live in below poverty line. Poverty is a brutal denial of Human rights. Poverty is a condition generated by chronic situations where people are deprived, often resulting in homelessness, inadequate education, poor health conditions, lack of opportunities for livelihood and inability to access public services indeed justice itself. Each of these conditions corresponds to the violation of internationally recognized Human Rights standards namely, the right to adequate housing, right to education, right to health, right to livelihood, the right to equal access to public services and right to seek justice, etc.

It is noted that several other Economic issues are closely linked to human rights. These include the equitable distribution of income and wealth, utilization of resources and intellectual property rights, conflicts between people and wild life, resettlement issues around development projects such as dams and mines, widening gap between the rich and the poor, the difference between the economically developed countries and the developing countries etc. Similarly, there are serious conflicts between the rights of rural communities for even basic resources such as water and the industrial sector that requires large amount of water for sustaining its productivity. The right to land or common property resources of tribal people is infringed upon by large development projects such as dams and mining. Movement to protect the right of indigenous people are growing worldwide.

Conclusion

In fact, in many ways observance of Human Rights is a vital step towards economic development. Because when people are denied their rights, it is often results in social instability, war and other conflicts which have serious economic consequences. Therefore, economic development agents must recognize that their investments and institutions become unproductive if people are denied their rights. Hence they should know the facts that Human Rights are important foundation for economic development. There has been some progress concerning human rights during the last few decades, still there are violation of these rights in some parts of the world. So we have to promote love for human rights and ensuring that all enjoy human rights. Finally I conclude my speech with the words 'live and let live'.

REFERENCES

1. Encyclopedia Britanica.
2. United Nations, Human Rights: A Compilation of International Instruments of the United Nations-1967.
3. Bharucha, Erach: UGC, Universities Press.
4. Paul James, C.N. : The Human Rights to Development: Its Meaning and Importance". Third World Legal Studies, Volume-II, Article-2, 199.

Human Rights Management after Globalization **Pages 146-150**
Edited by: **Dr. Rabi Narayana Misra**
ISBN: 978-93-88854-05-4
Edition: **2019**
Published by: **Discovery Publishing House Pvt. Ltd., New Delhi (India)**

Chapter 15

The Role of Civil Society in Protecting the Human Rights

[1]P. Aravind Swamy

Human rights are rights inherent to all human beings, whatever our nationality, place of residence, sex, national or ethnic origin, colour, religion, language, or any other status. We are all equally entitled to our human rights without discrimination. These rights are all interrelated, interdependent and indivisible. Universal human rights are often expressed and guaranteed by law, in the forms of treaties, customary international law, general principles and other sources of international law. International human rights law lays down obligations of Governments to act in certain ways or to refrain from certain acts, in order to promote and protect human rights and fundamental freedoms of individuals or groups.

Every day in every part of the world, civil society contributes to the promotion, protection and advancement of human rights. Whatever they call themselves — human rights defenders, human rights NGOs, bar associations, student clubs, trade unions, university institutes, bloggers, or charities working with discriminated groups - civil society actors work for a better future and share the common goals of justice, equality, and human dignity. A dynamic, diverse and independent civil society, able to operate freely, knowledgeable and skilled with regard to human rights, is a key element in securing sustainable human rights protection in all regions of the world.

The NGOs play important role to become a concrete expression of international, national and regional and local

[1] Lecturer in Economics, S.Ch.V.P.M.R. Govt. Degree College, Ganapavaram.

level voice to assist and stand up for those who can't speak themselves. They help the victims of human right violation by providing them assistance and advice. They file cases, writ petitions and public interest litigations on behalf of victims and public at large for protection of human rights. The NGOs have fought against the system of bonded labour, fake encounters by police, protection of women children's rights, custodian violence and custodian death, prevention of torture and other inhuman practices.

The civil societies and NGOs mobilise public opinion on various issues of national and international importance. They pressurize the government on certain issues such as protection of prisoners rights, torture etc. They approach the judiciary on behalf of poor people who otherwise have no access to justice.

At the international level, the status of human rights is watched by many NGOs. Amnesty International is one such organization. This organization is dedicated to publicizing violation of human rights, especially freedom of speech and religion and right to political dissent. It also works for the release of political prisoners and, when necessary, for the relief of their families. For the commendable services in human rights, Amnesty International was awarded the Noble Prize for peace in 1977. Other international NGOs such as Australia Asia Worker Links (AAWL) in Australia, Kenya college and the Legal Resources Centre (LRC) in South Africa, Cool Earth in UK, The Human Rights Foundation (HRF) in America are striving hard for the protection of human rights.

Australia Asia Worker Links (AAWL) is an Australian non-governmental organization active since 1979, established to forge international labour movement links in the Asia-Pacific region. AAWL supports union, human, indigenous and women rights, prompting solidarity between unions and advocating for improvements in corporate citizenship in the region. The Fred Hallows Foundation is a non-profit, community based, non-government development aid organization that focuses on treating and preventing blindness and other vision problems. It operates in Australia, The pacific, South and South East Asia and Africa.

Khanya College is an independent non-governmental organization based in Johannesburg, South Africa. Established in 1986, the primary aim of Khanya College is to assist various constituencies within working class and poor communities to respond to the challenges posed by the forces of economic and political globalization. The motto of the organization is "Education for Liberalization". The Legal Resources Centre (LRC) is a human rights organization based in Johannesburg, South Africa. It is safeguarding human rights by employing 65 lawyers specializing in public-interest law.

Cool Earth is another UK based international non-governmental organization that protects endangered rainforest to combat global warming, protect ecosystem and provide sustainable jobs for local people. Cool Earth protects and secures rainforest under imminent threat of destruction, working with other NGOs. The Human Rights Foundation (HRF) is an non-profit organization whose stated mission is "to ensure that freedom is both preserved and promoted" in the Americans. Its head office is in New York, USA. Its definition of human rights focuses on the essential ideals of freedom of self-determination and freedom from tyranny and the rights of property.

In India many NGOs like Sulabh Movement, Child Relief and You (CRY), Campaign Against Child Labour (CACL) etc., are actively involved in protecting human rights and capacity building activities. Sulabh movement is a major social movement in the country for the betterment and welfare of Dalits, in a generic sense, and in particular for the liberation and mainstreaming of scavengers. Child Relief and You (CRY) is a voluntary organization committed to the upliftment of millions of children who have been deprived of their childhood due to various reasons. Campaign Against Child labour (CACL) is a joint initiative of youth for Voluntary Action (YUVA), Pune and Tere des Hommes (Germany) India programme. The Campaign is currently supported by ILO and actively working for progressive eradication of child labour through provision of education, organisation of awareness programmes, promotion of legislative changes and rescuing children in bondage or victims of abuse.

Organisations like Saheli and Chetan are actively involved in the protection of Women's Rights. They provide free legal aid to women to fight for their rights against gender bias and child discrimination. Butterflies are an NGO with a programme for street children. It was started in 1988 and its activities include non-formal education, saving schemes for children, vocational training, holding Bal Sabhas, creating awareness for children's rights and networking with other NGOS and research and documentation. People's Union for Civil Liberties (PUCL) is a prominent civil rights organization formed by veteran socialist and campaign leader Jaya Prakashnarayana. Its main aim is to bring those concerned about defending civil liberties and human rights from different backgrounds onto a common platform.

Peoples Union for Democratic Rights came into existence in 1976-77 as the Delhi unit of a large national forum, and became PUDR on 1 February, 1981. In the last two and a half decades of existence the organisation has taken up hundreds of instances of violations of democratic rights, covering most parts of the country and involving the rights of many section of the society. PUDR conducts investigations, issue statements, distribute leaflets, organizes public meetings, demonstrations and dharnas and fights legal casesto highlight the violation of people's rights, and to help towards their redressal.

Bandhu Mukti Morcha (BMM) or Bonded Labour Liberation Front (BLLF) is a non-governmental organisation in India working to end bonded labour. BBMs efforts are credited with the passing of legislation to abolish child labour in India (The Child Labour (Prohibition and Regulation) Act, 1986).

The following are some examples in which NGO take an action in court for protecting human rights in india:

- Visaka and Others Vs. State of Rajastan & Others.
- People's Union for Democratic Rights Vs. State of Bihar & Others (19 December, 1986).

- Bandhumukti Morcha Vs. Union of India & Others (16 December, 1983).
- Sahelivs Commissioner of Police.
- People's Union for Democratic Rights Vs. Police Commissioner Delhi, Headquarters 1989, 4 SCC, 730.

Undoubtedly NGOs are playing prominent role in protecting human rights all over the world. But there are certain short comings that are to be overcome. NGOs need to expand their programmes, campaigns, skits from yearly or bi-yearly to monthly. Frequent programmes increase the awareness of human rights even more than yearly. They also need to get more aid both from foreign and within India which will be useful to carry out their cause. They must have clear goals and priorities, they should define what they are trying to achieve as clearly as possible. They should think strategically and assess how short term goals fit in with long term ones. NGOs must have a clear written work plan for both individuals and staff activities. Plan reminds people of what the goals are, it helps keep things on track and with major projects or campaigns it helps people see where they fit into bog picture.

Key words: Universal human rights, civil societies, public interest litigations, inhuman practices.

REFERENCES

1. http://www. collegeessayshelp. com/blog/2014/09/essay-sample-on-the-role-of-ngos-in-protecting-human-rights/#sthash. zNBVSLpG. dpuf.
2. www.humanrights.com/voices-for-human-rights/human-rights- organization/non- governmental.html.
3. Human Rights in India Dr. Sunil Deshat and Pratap Singh Allahabad lawAgency - law publishers, p. no. 120.
4. Section 2{d} of the Human Rights Act, 1993.
5. Subleterns-a quarterly Newsletter of Indian Social Institute, New Delhi, vol. 20 April-June 2012 article by Archana Singh p. no. 3.
6. Justice A.D Mane's Lectures on Human Rights Edited by Dr. Vijay N. Ghormade Hind Law House-2007 Edition p. no. 325.
7. An Introduction to Human Rights by Dr. Vijay Chitins, p.no. 10.

Human Rights Management after Globalization **Pages 151-153**
Edited by: Dr. Rabi Narayana Misra
ISBN: 978-93-88854-05-4
Edition: 2019
Published by: Discovery Publishing House Pvt. Ltd., New Delhi (India)

Chapter 16

Are Human Rights Needed when Human is Being in Human

[1]Dr. J. Sanath Kumar

Now-a-days, there is a fashion to use some words or terms like 'right to education', 'right to information' and 'right to protest peacefully' frequently. Many a times, we feel that we have certain human rights with the influence of others.

Do we really know what does the term 'rights' mean? Rights are rules of interaction between people. They place constraints and obligations upon the actions of the state and individuals or groups. For example, if one has a right to live, this means that rest does not have the liberty to kill others. Rights are defined as claims of an individual that are essential for the development of one's own self and that are recognized by society.

When a human behaves as inhuman in society some rules, regulations and control mechanism are imposed by governments, institutions organized by human beings. Again some human beings raise voice against these rules and restrictions as human rights. The situation itself creates by human beings against human beings. When a human behaves or acts as human being this situation would not have rise.

Human being is a kind of creature who is basically governed by his appetite, needs, interest, emotions, and passions. Being human is when the same human being uses his conscience, love, care, empathy to govern his appetite, needs, interests, emotions, passions for the greater change of his life and his surroundings.

[1] Principal, RRDS Govt. Degree College, Bhimavaram.

It is very difficult to define the human right as there is no universally acceptable conception of it. Each individual must have some rights not only to survive in the community but also to make the life better. Some observes that "human rights are the rights that everyone has, and everyone equally, by virtue of their very humanity". Rights are often considered fundamental to civilization, being regarded as established pillars of society and culture.

To ensure the economic interest of the human being, UNO also provides certain economic rights as human rights such as:

1. Right to social security.
2. Right to food, health and adequate standard of living.

To implement this recently Government of India banned ₹ 500 and ₹ 1000 currency notes, but it had given some inconvenience. This situation rose as against to human rights by human activists. They argued that there were 87 deaths connected to demonetization. People have been made to stand in queues for hours, even days, outside banks and ATMs to access their own money as if it were charity. Weddings have been cancelled due to the cash crunch. Small and marginal businesses, who largely rely on cash transactions, have suffered a massive drop in trade. Farmers, in the middle of the sowing season, are unable to pay for seeds, fertilizers, other farm inputs or access loans. Patients, including infants and the chronically ill, have been denied treatment. Travel, both domestic and foreign, has been disrupted. Daily wage earners, agriculture labour, migrant and informal workers and contract workers, are some of the worst hit by this move, unable to earn a wage or use their savings. Women, children, the elderly and persons with disabilities are particularly vulnerable and face the severity of this move acutely. Every day, new tragedies unfold. All this brought about by just an executive order, without even the courtesy of an ordinance.

We are always talking about rights but not duties. Whereas Fundamental Rights are justifiable, the Fundamental Duties are non-justifiable. Introduction of fake Currency, Black Marketing, Currency Storage, Corruption, supporting to terrorist organizations, anti-national activities are all inhuman things. These inhuman activities of some people causes and disturbs of other human rights.

But the rights have real meaning only if individuals perform duties. A duty is something that someone is expected or required to do. In fact, rights and duties are two wheels on which the chariot of life moves forward smoothly. Life can become smoother if rights and duties go hand in hand and be complementing to each other. Rights are what we want others to do for us whereas the duties are those acts which we should perform for others. Thus, a right comes with an obligation to show respect for the rights of others. The obligations that accompany rights are in the form of duties.

Human Rights Management after Globalization **Pages 154-158**
Edited by: Dr. Rabi Narayana Misra
ISBN: 978-93-88854-05-4
Edition: 2019
Published by: Discovery Publishing House Pvt. Ltd., New Delhi (India)

Chapter 17

Forces Influencing Human Rights in India

[1]Dr. G. Swathi
[2]G. Tirumala Vasu Deva Rao

Abstract

Human rights are vital part of human being both male and female exist in it but our social system makes differences between them. So a big fight takes place for human dignity. Human rights are often examined only within the scope of law. It is true that legal provisions are essential to claim any right, including human rights, but perhaps mere legal provisions are not enough to understand, protect and promote human rights in most societies.

Even though the general framework, philosophy and perception of human rights should be universal, the crucial point is, can we really understand the scope and dimensions of human rights without considering the concerned society and culture? Can society, culture and economy be neutral? These questions bring out the issue of holistic understanding of human rights. Anthropology with its holistic approach can contribute significantly in understanding the causes and factors of human rights violations and strengthening the forces of struggle for promoting and protecting human rights at different levels of society. After decades of mobilization and advocacy, how familiar are ordinary people with human rights, and how is this familiarity shaped by socio-economic status? We explore these questions with new data from the Human Rights Perception Polls, representative surveys conducted in four countries. We find that public exposure to the term "human rights" is high in

[1] Lecturer in Zoology, Govt. Degree College for Women, Srikalahasthi.
[2] Lecturer in History, Govt. Degree College, Nagari.

Colombia, Mexico and parts of Morocco, but more moderate in and around Mumbai, India. The public's rate of personal contact with rights activists, workers and volunteers, however, is much more limited. For both indicators, moreover, socio-economic status is a meaningful statistical predictor. People who are more educated, wealthier, reside in urban areas and enjoy Internet access also tend to be more familiar with the term "human rights," and to have met a human rights worker, activist, or volunteer. These findings should concern human rights strategists keen to promote ties with the poor. To address this challenge, human rights groups should develop more popularly oriented models of engagement and resource mobilization. There is direct relationship between Socio-economic status and utilization of human rights in India.

Keywords: Human rights, legal provisions, Socio-economic status.

Introduction

Human behaviour is conceived of as an outcome of genetic and biochemical characteristics, past learning experiences, motivational states, psycho-social antecedents, and the cultural context in which it unfolds [1] Culture plays a complex role in the natural history and psycho-social development of human behaviour [2] comprising of customs, beliefs, values, knowledge and skills. [3] Social norms, the shared rules that specify appropriate and inappropriate behaviours; [4] mores, that people consider vital to their well-being and to their most cherished values, [5] and sanctions, the socially imposed rewards and punishments that compel people to comply with norms [6] constitute important ingredients of a culture. Orlandi *et al.* (1992), [2] define culture as shared values, beliefs, norms, traditions, customs, art, history, folklore and institutions of a group of people. A society which is a cohesive group of people shares all the ingredients of the culture among its members.

The Indian sub-continent has been likened to a deep net into which various races and people have drifted and been caught in the remote past and their diverse origins have dictated variety. Geographical conditions of the sub-continent forced these varied people to stay together in a multiple society imposing on them what has been described by historians as 'Unity in Diversity' having cultural homogeneity.[7]

Stigmatization

Social stigma refers to a 'defect' in a person's social identity-negative information about a person that is known by others. In the traditional Hindu social hierarchy an untouchable is evaluated so low that the depth of degradation accords him a sub-human status. [8] Negative reactions from others may take many forms-ranging from disinterest, criticism, prejudice, avoidance, rejection, betrayal, Stigmatization, ostracism, abandonment and abuse to bullying. [9] On account of the stigmatized existence, a deprived caste student is highly self-conscious, sensitive to others' comments and criticism, has real or imagined evaluation, and is likely to feel socially anxious, especially when under observationa. [10] The psychological core of all instances is the stigma in which a person is the recipient of negative reactions.

Social Change and Individual Role

A role is the part that a person plays within the given social context. [11] Associated with each role is a set of expectations regarding the appropriate behaviour of the occupant for that role. A stable society has clear role definitions, while the social change burdens the individual with new role demands. Role novelty occurs when a person finds himself in a position he has not previously occupied and while playing a new role, he may be unaware of which behaviour he perceives to be appropriate. [12] This is a common source of one's uncertainty about self-presentation and triggers social anxiety. [13]

In the traditional Hindu society everyone has an explicitly defined social role. Members of the erstwhile low castes were assigned the role of serving the members of higher castes. With the advent of modern education, urbanization, and new technologies, there has been a massive occupational mobility from the traditionally hateful and defiling occupations to the newly created respectable white-collar positions, the first-generation educated deprived finds him in a new role with many psychological difficulties. Motivation for change is an important factor for altering behaviour pattern and a person is more likely to adjust to the change if he perceives the change to be desirable.

Reaction to Discrimination, Rejection

Human-beings are acutely responsive to how and what other people perceive, evaluate and feel about them. Positive and negative reactions from others often affect the quality of interpersonal relationship. [14] Behavioural scientists have documented that positive responses from others foster a psychological and physical well-being, whereas, long-term exposure to negative reactions is associated with psychological difficulties and poor physical health. [15, 16]

People who experience rejection generally have three sets of motives. The first motive involves a heightened desire for social connections, those who can possibly provide acceptance and support; the second set of motives involves angry, anti-social urges to defend oneself or to hurt the source of rejection; third, the rejected people are motivated to avoid further rejection, therefore withdraw themselves. Members of India's deprived castes often crave for establishing social connections with the members of privileged castes and wish to gain their acceptance, and when they fail in doing so anger and hostility generates. Anger and aggression are common responses to rejection and often lead to long-lasting break in social bonds. [17] Studies have shown aggressive behaviour among rejected school children by their peer group. [18] Anger and aggression in rejected children occurs as a result of pain or frustration associated with rejection. [19] Moreover, rejection by the peer group not only creates a great deal of suffering in the child, but also predicts negative emotional and behavioural outcomes in the future. [20]

Rejected people may withdraw from and avoid interpersonal interactions, not only with those who rejected them but often with other people as well. They may either physically leave the situation or withdraw socially and psychologically, while remaining physically present when they cannot escape or avoid social encounter. [21] The events that connote rejection immediately elicit negative emotions, such as, sadness, loneliness, hurt, anger, jealousy, [17] and lower self-esteem in the victims. India's deprived castes who perceive rejection from the majority groups breed negative emotions, low self-esteem, avoidance behaviour and aggressive traits among their members.

REFERENCES

1. Sutker P. Drug and Psychopathology. Maryland: National Institute of Drug Abuse Research. 1977:19:23-8.
3. Linton R. New York: Apple-tone; 1947. The Study of Man; pp. 132-40.
4. Berne E. New York: Newton Books; 1964. Games People Play: The Psychology of Human Relationship.
5. Bellah RN, Madsen R, Sullivan WM, Swindler A, Tipton SM. New York: Harper and Row; 1985. Habits of the Heart.
6. Light D, Jr, Keller S. New York: Knopf; 1985. Sociology.
9. Leary MR, Koch E, Hechenbleikner N. Emotional Responses to Interpersonal Rejection. In: Leary MR, Editor. Interpersonal Rejection. New York: Oxford University Press; 2001. pp. 145-6.
10. Williams KD. New York: Guilford Press; 2001. Ostracism: The Power of Silence.
12. Goodman N. 2nd edition. New York: Crowell Collier; 1964. Race Awareness in Young Children. Cambridge Hass: Addition Wesely 1952.
13. Marc R, Learn M.R. Beverly Hills London: Sage Publications; 1963. Understanding Social Anxiety: Social Personality and Clinical Perspective.
14. Buckley KE, Winkel RE, Leary M., Jr Reaction to Acceptance and Rejection: Effect of Level and Sequence of Relational Evaluation. J Exp Soc Psychol. 2004; 40: 14-28.
15. Pressman S, Cohen S. Does Positive Affect Influence Health? Psycholog Bull. 2005:131:925-71. [PubMed]
16. Williams DR, Neighbors HW, Jackson JS. Racial/ethnic Discrimination and Health: Findings from Community Studies. Am J Public Health. 2003 ;93: 200-8. [PMCfree article] [PubMed]
17. MacDonald, Leary MR. Why does Social Exclusion Hurt. The Relationship between Social and Physical Pain? Psychol Bull. 2005:131:202-23. [PubMed]
18. Kupersmidt JB, Burchinal M, Patterson CJ. Developmental Patterns of Childhood Peer Relations as Predictors of Externalizing Behavour Problems. Deve Psychopathol. 1995;7:825-43.
19. Bettencourt BA, Tally A, Benjamin AJ, Valentine J. Personality and Aggressive Behavior under Provoking and Neutral Conditions: A Meta-analytic Review. Psychol Bull. 2006:132:751-77. [PubMed]

Human Rights Management after Globalization **Pages 159-162**
Edited by: Dr. Rabi Narayana Misra
ISBN: 978-93-88854-05-4
Edition: 2019
Published by: Discovery Publishing House Pvt. Ltd., New Delhi (India)

Chapter 18

Human Rights Vs. Women Rights

[1]T. Sreevaram
[2]Dr. R.N. Misra

Every human-being is entitled to certain rights and freedom irrespective of their origin, ethnicity, race, colour, nationality, citizenship, sex or religion. These rights are considered universal for humanity. The principal objective of both Indian and international laws is to protect the human personality and its fundamental rights. These are the rights which are inherent in all citizens, because of their being human. Indian constitution guaranteesus with six fundamental rights *viz.*, right to equality, freedom, right against exploitation, freedom of religion, culture and educational rights.

Human rights are aimed at preserving the dignity of people, one cannot call a society a good and a just society until all its citizens enjoy these human rights. The human rights laws aim at eliminating unjust discrimination against any human being. The concept of human right is based on the principle of human solidarity, cooperation and development. The impact and importance of human rights are so deep and strong that the constitution of India incorporated many of the provisions of rights codified in its constitution. This may be treated as land mark in the history of progress of civilization.

The charter of human rights exerts tremendous pressure on all political authorities. Strong vigilance is noticed throughout world against the violation of human rights.

[1] Lacturer in of Chemistry, Govt. Degree College, Ravulapalem, A.P.
[2] Prof. MBA, SMGT Berhampur, Odisha.

Women Rights

Although not a numerical minority, women have often faced the same kinds of barriers as African Americans and other racial minorities in their quest for equal political, economic and social opportunities in India.

Women have fought - in the courts and the legislatures, as well as in the streets and the forums of public opinion - for the right to vote, to hold property, to be elected to public office, to gain an education, to hold certain kinds of jobs, to receive pay equal to men, girl child abuse, honour killings etc. In addition, women face unique kinds of discrimination based on gender, such as sexual harassment and job discrimination.

In recent years the principal civil rights issues for women have centered primarily on employment and education. The fight for women's equal opportunity has been number of fronts: the successful enactment of the Equal Pay,equal amendments and family and medical act. But, women have found that simply passing legislation without accompanying enforcement does little to dismantle the obstacles to equal opportunity.

The issue of women empowerment and inequality have been taken up as a human rights issue. Several institutions, organizations are working hard to create awareness among the masses. It is high time that the society has come forward in support women in her fight for justice. She should be treated at par with men all venues of social framework. Her position need to be elevated.

Violence against women commonly known as gender-based discrimination and violence refers to violent acts committed against women. Violence against women is very common especially in developing third world countries like India. Even in developed and modern nations still today gender-based violence is not totally eliminated and still exists though comparatively the rate is lower than the underdeveloped and/or developing countries. It has spread like a plague that has engulfed and destroyed many homes and families and a situation that needs to be addressed with complete focus as a healthy society produces healthy generations which in turn results in healthy and prosperous nations.

The most effective way to reduce tolerance towards violence against women is to openly debate the subject as still there is limited knowledge regarding most workable interventions for the prevention of gender-based violations.

Status of Women in India

One of the vital concerns in India is the discrimination between genders. The status of women in the ancient Indian society was quite better however in the middle age it got deteriorated. Various ill practices came into existence against women which deteriorated the women status. Indian society became male dominated society and women were started to be treated as man's slaves. At some place in the country, women are still ill-treated by the men even after the fast changes in the society. Earlier the elders of the family were not be happy on the birth of a female child in the home however they became double happy if the child was male. They understood that male child will be source of money whereas female child will be consumer of money. Birth of daughter was supposed as curse to the family. The gradual positive changes in the Indian society has been proved to be beneficial for the women status. Positive thinking of people has taken a swift speed which has changed human mind politically, economically and socially towards women.

Women status was started changing after many years of struggle for India's freedom when Mahatma Gandhi gave a call to women to come forward and take part in the independence movement. There is hand of many great women like Vijaya Laxmi Pandit, Sarojini Naidu, Mrs. Aruna Asaf Ali, etc. who helped in changing the women status in India. After the occurrence of Mrs. Indira Gandhi as a Prime Minister of India, the condition of women was changed positively a lot. Later the prestigious positions of many women in India has proved that women are not inferior to men and can go together.

Muslim[1] Women in India are one of the major groups deprived of their equality within the Human right framework[2]. Their hardship has derived from cultural and religious reasons where the functions of a woman concerning family matters are seen as less than half, according to hijabs, then that of their male counterparts[3].

Even today, there are several instances of human rights violation at various places of the world. There can be no permanent and regular prosperity of a nation unless every country creates such conditions in which human rights are enjoyed by its natives.

REFRENCES

1. Syed Mehartaj Bejum Human Rights in India: Issues and Perspectives (2000, A.P.H. Publishing Corporation, New Delhi) at 188.
2. Jump up to : a, b, c, d, e at 188.
3. Jump upto : a, b, c, d at 190.

Human Rights Management after Globalization **Pages 163-167**
Edited by: Dr. Rabi Narayana Misra
ISBN: 978-93-88854-05-4
Edition: 2019
Published by: Discovery Publishing House Pvt. Ltd., New Delhi (India)

Chapter 19

Constitutional and Legal Rights to Women in India

[1]R.J.L.P. Priyanka, III BA

Introduction

Human Rights are rights inherent to all human beings irrespective of their Nationality, place of residence, sex, religion, race, colour, language etc. The constitution of India also guarantees the equality of rights of men and women. In order to uphold and implement the constitutional mandate, the state has enacted various laws and taken various measures indented to ensure equal rights, check social discrimination and various forms of violence and atrocities on women. The rights available to women in India can be classified into two categories. 1. Constitutional Rights, 2. Legal Rights. Constitutional rights are those which are provided in the various provisions of the constitution. On the other hand legal rights are those which are provided in the various laws or acts of the parliament and state legislatures.

Constitutional Rights to Women

The following are the rights and safeguards enshrined in the constitution for women in India:

1. The state shall not discriminate against any citizen of India on the ground of sex.
2. The state is empowered to make any special provision for women. In other words, this provision enables the state to make affirmative discrimination in favour of women.

[1] Govt. Degree College, Ravulapalem.

3. No citizen shall be discriminated against or be ineligible for any employment or office under the state on the ground of sex.
4. Traffic in human beings and forced labour is prohibited.
5. The state to secure for men and women equally the right to an adequate means of livelihood.
6. The state to secure equal pay for equal work for both Indian men and women.
7. The state is required to ensure that the health and strength of women workers are not abused and that they are not forced by economic necessity to enter avocations unsuited to their strength.
8. The state shall make provision for securing just and humane conditions of work and maternity relief.
9. It shall be the duty of every citizen of India to renounce practices derogatory to the dignity of women.
10. One-third of the total number of seats to be filled by direct election in every Panchayat shall be reserved for women.
11. One-third of the total number of offices of chairpersons in the Panchayats at each level shall be reserved for women.
12. One-third of the total number of seats to be filled by direct election in every Municipality shall be reserved for women.
13. The offices of chairpersons in the Municipalities shall be reserved for women in such manner as the State Legislature may provide.

Legal Rights to Women

The following are the various laws and acts passed by the parliament and state legislatures for women:

1. Protection of Women from Domestic Violence Act (2005) is a comprehensive legislation to protect women in India from all forms of domestic violence. It also covers women who have been/are in a relationship with the abuser and are subjected to violence of any kind—physical, sexual, mental, verbal or emotional.

2. Immoral Traffic (Prevention) Act (1956) is the premier legislation for prevention of trafficking for commercial sexual exploitation. In other words, it prevents trafficking in women and girls for the purpose of prostitution as an organised means of living.
3. Indecent Representation of Women (Prohibition) Act (1986) prohibits indecent representation of women through advertisements or in publications, writings, paintings, figures or in any other manner.
4. Commission of Sati (Prevention) Act (1987) provides for the more effective prevention of the commission of sati and its glorification on women.
5. Dowry Prohibition Act (1961) prohibits the giving or taking of dowry at or before or any time after the marriage from women.
6. Maternity Benefit Act (1961) regulates the employment of women in certain establishments for certain period before and after child-birth and provides for maternity benefit and certain other benefits.
7. Medical Termination of Pregnancy Act (1971) provides for the termination of certain pregnancies by registered medical practitioners on humanitarian and medical grounds.
8. Pre-Conception and Pre-Natal Diagnostic Techniques (Prohibition of Sex Selection) Act (1994) prohibits sex selection before or after conception and prevents the misuse of pre-natal diagnostic techniques for sex determination leading to female foeticide.
9. Equal Remuneration Act (1976) provides for payment of equal remuneration to both men and women workers for same work or work of a similar nature. It also prevents discrimination on the ground of sex, against women in recruitment and service conditions.
10. Dissolution of Muslim Marriages Act (1939) grants a Muslim wife the right to seek the dissolution of her marriage.

11. Muslim Women (Protection of Rights on Divorce) Act (1986) protects the rights of Muslim women who have been divorced by or have obtained divorce from their husbands.
12. Family Courts Act (1984) provides for the establishment of Family Courts for speedy settlement of family disputes.
13. Indian Penal Code (1860) contains provisions to protect Indian women from dowry death, rape, kidnapping, cruelty and other offences.
14. Code of Criminal Procedure (1973) has certain safeguards for women like obligation of a person to maintain his wife, arrest of woman by female police and so on.
15. Indian Christian Marriage Act (1872) contain provisions relating to marriage and divorce among the Christian community.
16. Legal Services Authorities Act (1987) provides for free legal services to Indian women.
17. Hindu Marriage Act (1955) introduced monogamy and allowed divorce on certain specified grounds. It provided equal rights to Indian man and woman in respect of marriage and divorce.
18. Hindu Succession Act (1956) recognizes the right of women to inherit parental property equally with men.
19. Minimum Wages Act (1948) does not allow discrimination between male and female workers or different minimum wages for them.
20. Mines Act (1952) and Factories Act (1948) prohibits the employment of women between 7 P.M. to 6 A.M. in mines and factories and provides for their safety and welfare.
21. The following other legislation's also contain certain rights and safeguards for women:
    1. Indian Divorce Act (1869).
    2. Parsi Marriage and Divorce Act (1936).

3. Special Marriage Act (1954).
4. Foreign Marriage Act (1969).
5. Hindu Adoptions and Maintenance Act (1956).

22. National Commission for Women Act (1990) provided for the establishment of a National Commission for Women to study and monitor all matters relating to the constitutional and legal rights and safeguards of women.
23. Sexual Harassment of Women at Workplace (Prevention, Prohibition and Redressal). Act (2013) provides protection to women from sexual harassment at all workplaces both in public and private sector, whether organised or unorganized.

Conclusion

Thus there are several constitutional and legal rights to women. Even though there are various constitutional provisions and legislations contain several rights and safeguards for women, it has been found that each and every right of women is being violated in one or another form. The crime against women in India is increasing at a faster rate. The National Crime Records Bureau (NCRB) had predicted that growth rate of crime against women would be higher than the population growth by 2010, which was found to be true. A total of 3,27,394 cases of crime against women were reported in the country during 2015. The crime rate under crimes agasint women was reported as 53.9 in the same period. Now the question arises whether the laws ensures that women get their rights? And that their human rights are protected? There is still a long way to go to answer such queations.

REFERENCES

1. https://edugeneral.org/blog/polity/women-rights-in-india/
2. Crime in India-2015, NCRB, Ministry of Home Affairs.

Human Rights Management after Globalization **Pages 168-172**
Edited by: Dr. Rabi Narayana Misra
ISBN: 978-93-88854-05-4
Edition: 2019
Published by: Discovery Publishing House Pvt. Ltd., New Delhi (India)

Chapter 20

Women and Human Rights in India

[1]M. Swarnalatha, M.A., M.Phil.

Abstract

Human rights are rights inherent to all human beings irrespective of their Nationality, place of residence, sex, religion, race, colour, language etc. Human rights are as old as human civilisation, but their use and relevance have been well defined during the recent years. The constitution of India also guarantees the equality of rights of men and women. Women are emotionally stronger than men. Undoubtedly women endure much more pain than man do. No men do go through even half the pain a women goes through during labour. Margaret Thatcher, Benazir Bhutto and Indira Gandhi have shown that women can rule a country even better than man. However women have not been treated nicely by men all throughout the time. They have been denied their rights. Even though there are various legislations contain several rights and safeguards for women, it has been found that each and every right of women is being violated in one or another way. The crimes against women in India are increasing at a faster rate. The main objective of the presentation of this seminar paper is to study the various crimes done against women in India.

Key words: Human rights, Constitution of India, Crimes against women.

Introduction

Human rights are as old as human civilisation, but their use and relevance have been well defined during the recent years.

[1] Lecturer in Economics, Govt. Degree College, Tadepalligudem.

The constitution of India also guarantees the equality of rights of men and women. According to Article-14 'the state shall not deny to any person equality before law or the equal protection of laws within the territory of India'. Also Article-15 states 'state shall not discriminate against any citizen on grounds only of religion, race, caste, sex, place of birth, or any of them'. The rights available to women in India can be classified into two categories namely constitutional rights and legal rights. The constitutional rights are those, which are provided in the various provisions of the constitution. The legal rights, on the other hand, are those which are provided in the various laws of the parliament and state legislations. But in reality, in the sphere of women's human rights in India, there exist a wide gap between theory and practice. The main objective of the presentation of this seminar paper is to study the various crimes done against women in India.

Crimes Against Women in India

Woman is being exploited in India from the early times in the form of devadasis, jauhar, pardah, sati, child marriage etc. Discrimination against girl child starts at the moment when she enters into the mother's womb. The child is exposed to gender differences since birth and even recent times, even before birth in the form of sex determination tests, leading to foeticide and female infanticide. If a girl child opens her eyes in any way, she is killed after her birth by different cruel methods in some parts of the country. The principle of gender equality is enshrined in the constitution of India. In order to uphold and implement the constitutional mandate, the state has enacted various laws and taken measures intended to ensure equal rights, check social discrimination and various forms of violence and atrocities on women. Although women may be the victims of any of the general crimes such as murder, robbery, cheating etc., only the crimes which are directed specifically against women *i.e.*, gender specific crimes are characterized as crimes against women. Various new legislations have been brought and amendments have been made in existing laws with a view to handle the crimes effectively. Despite efforts to raise the social status of women for more than a century, India still ranks 118 among 177 nations on gender equity. Even though there are various legislations contain several rights and safeguards for women, it has been found that each and every right of the women is being violated in one or another way. The crimes against women in India are increasing at a faster rate. The National Crime Records Bureau (NCRB) had predicted that growth rate of crime against women would be higher than the population growth by 2010, which was found to be true. The main objective of the presentation of this seminar paper is to study the various crimes done against women in India:

1. *Crimes Against Women:* A total of 3,27,394 cases of crime against women (both under various sections of Indian Penal Code and special local laws) were reported in the country during the year 2015. These crimes have been continuously increased during 2011-2014 with 2,28,650 cases in 2011, which further increased to 2,44,270 cases in 2012 and 3,09,546 cases in 2013 to 3,37,922 cases in 2014. Of course there is a marginal decline in 2015. The crime rate under crimes against women was reported as 53.9 in 2015.
2. *Rape*: In rape cases, it is very torturing that the victim has to prove that she has been raped. The victim finds it difficult to undergo medical examination immediately after the trauma of assault. Besides this, the family too is reluctant to bring in prosecution due to family prestige and hard police procedures. However a total of 34,651 cases of rape were registered during 2015. Out of which 557 were incest rape and 95 were custodial rape. In addition to these, a total of 4437 cases were registered under attempt to commit rape during 2015.
3. *Abduction of Women:* Abduction of women is another crime against women. A total of 59,277 cases were registered under kidnapping and abduction of women during 2015. These cases have shown an increase of 3.4% during 2015 over the previous year Of the total cases, Delhi has reported highest crime rate of 46.3 compared to the national average of 9.8.

4. *Dowry Cases:* In spite of the Dowry prohibition Act passed by the government, which has made dowry demands in wedding illegal, the dowry incidents are increasing day by day. A total of 7,634 dowry death cases were registered in the country during the year 2015. Of the total cases of the dowry deaths, 30.6% of cases were reported in UP. In addition to the dowry death cases, a total of 9,894 cases were booked in 2015 under the dowry prohibition act. Maximum such cases were reported again in UP.
5. *Assault on Women with Intent to Outrage her Modesty:* Incidence of assault on women with intent to outrage her modesty, in the country have increased by 0.2% (from 82,238 cases in 2014 to 82,422 cases in 2015) during 2015 over the previous year.
6. *Cruelty by Husband or his Relatives:* A total of 1,13,103 cases were booked in 2015 under the cruelty by husband or his relatives in the country. Most of these cases were reported in West Bengal.
7. *Immoral Traffic of Women:* Immoral Traffic Prevention Act was passed in 1956, yet cases of immoral trafficking of young girls and women have been increasing. There are 2424 cases were registered during the year 2015.
8. *Domestic Violence:* Domestic Violence is undoubtedly a human right issue where it is very important to know what actually leads to act of domestic violence. The most common causes for women stalking and battering include: exploitation of women for demanding more dowry, discrimination of women, alienation of women's self acquired property fraudulently, torture by husband and in-laws of the husband, arguing with the partner, refusing to have sex with the partner, neglecting children, going out of home without telling the partner, not cooking properly or on time, indulging in extra marital affairs, not looking after in-laws, cruelty by husband or in-laws mentally or physically, abusing & insulting by using vulgar language, sexual harassment,

molestation, immoral traffic, rape, sodomy and all other inhuman acts. In all above stated causes women are subjected to torture and will be considered as the aggrieved person. Usually violence takes place due to lack of understandings between the couple as well as in the family. Although The Protection of Women from Domestic Violence Act, 2005, came into force on October 26th, 2006 yet the incidence of domestic violence is higher. A total of 461 cases were registered under this act during 2015, showing an increase of 8.2% over the previous year.

Conclusion

Thus all these violence done against women raises the question mark that how these special rights being given to women are helping them? What are the benefits of framing of such laws for women? Are they really helping them? Will the women really be given the equal status one day? All these questions are still unanswered. There is still a long way to go to answer such questions.

REFERENCES

1. Crime in India-2015, NCRB, Ministry of Home Affairs
2. RITU DHANOA, 'Violation of Women Human Rights in India', International Journal in Multidisciplinary and Academic Research (SSIJMAR) Vol. I, No. 4, November-December.
3. www.Best Current Affairs.com.

Human Rights Management after Globalization **Pages 173-181**
Edited by: Dr. Rabi Narayana Misra
ISBN: 978-93-88854-05-4
Edition: 2019
Published by: Discovery Publishing House Pvt. Ltd., New Delhi (India)

Chapter 21

Human Rights in India

[1]Dr. P. Sunanda Vijaya Lakshmi
[2]Amnuta Rani Misra

"All human beings are born free and equal in dignity and rights". So stated Article 1 of the Universal Declaration of Human Rights in 1948. This is what the Indians have been preaching since times immemorial as it has become the immemorial customs of our nation. Human Rights are a fundamental value. There is a long Indian tradition of standing up for the weak against abuse by the strong. Upholding human rights values in every aspect is firmly in our tradition. The "Great Mauryan emperor Ashoka the great renounced the path of violence after the massacre in the war of Kalinga". The "Great Moghul," Akbar the Great granted religious minorities legal status in his realm, One of the most influential was Mahatma Gandhi's movement to free his native India from British rule. It is the core of our Constitution and the heart of our national interest today. But the values that we stand for - freedom, human rights, the rule of law - are all universal values. Given the choice, people all over the world want them. But it is regretting that India who was once looked up by whole world as the pioneer of these values is now groveling in lowly dust of atrocities and human rights abuse. Human rights abuse is sadly a reality in Indian society, it is not just an affront to the values of tolerance, freedom and justice that underpin our society. It is also a tragic waste of human potential.

[1] Deptt. of Commerce, Government College (A) Rajamundry, Andhra Pradesh.

[2] Lecture in English, Mumbai.

The Need for Human Rights Education

The importance of human rights education hardly requires any over emphasis. It has a crucial role in preventing human rights violations from occurring.

The United Nations proclaimed that human rights education is "training, dissemination and information efforts aimed at the building of a universal culture of human rights through imparting knowledge and skills and the moulding of attitudes". These efforts are designed to strengthen respect for human rights and fundamental freedoms, facilitate the full development of human personality, sense of dignity, promote understanding, respect, gender equality and friendship to enable all persons to participate effectively in a free society, and further activities for maintenance of peace.

Human rights education, training and public information are, therefore, necessary and essential for the promotion and achievement of stable and harmonious relations among the communities and for fostering mutual understanding, tolerance and peace. Through the learning of human rights as a way of life, fundamental change could be brought about to eradicate poverty, ignorance, prejudices and discrimination based on sex, caste, religion and disability and other status amongst the people.

Human Rights Education in India

It may be said that in India that the content of human rights education is not different to what was taught by way of religion, be it Hinduism, Buddhism, Christianity or Islam, There is lot of truth in that statement. The quintessence of human rights is also the basic essence of all religions, Love, compassion, loving kindness are the same. However, while teaching religions we confined the obligations arising from these doctrines only to their followers. Human rights could bring in a universal aspect to moral and ethical education. And we in our divided societies are in great need of this on the other hand in the context of rapid secularization we could still retain a basic common ground for respect for each other. We could still be our brothers' keepers and withstand value systems which only promote selfish ways of life.

Indian textbooks barely mention human rights. Indirect references to human rights are included in the Directive Principles of the Constitution of India and in civics and history textbooks. Most universities in India do not offer human rights education, although some have three-month to one-year post-graduate courses on human rights. Section 12(h) of the Protection of Human Rights Act, 1993, requires the Commission to spread human rights literacy among various sections of society and promote awareness. The National Human Rights Commission of India and many NGOs have launched a countrywide public information campaign for human rights. It aims to make everyone more conscious of human rights and fundamental freedoms and better equipped to stand up for them. At the same time, the campaign spreads knowledge of the means which exist at the international and national levels to promote and protect human rights and fundamental freedoms.

What is Human Rights Education

Simply put, human rights education is all learning that develops the knowledge, skills and values of human rights.

The United Nations Decade for Human Rights Education (1995-2004) has defined Human Rights Education as "training, dissemination, and information efforts aimed at the building of a universal culture of human rights through the imparting of knowledge and skills and the molding of attitudes which are directed to:

(*a*) The strengthening of respect for human rights and fundamental freedoms;

(*b*) The full development of the human personality and the sense of its dignity;

(*c*) The promotion of understanding, respect, gender equality, and friendship among all nations, indigenous peoples and racial, national, ethnic, religious and linguistic groups;

(*d*) The enabling of all persons to participate effectively in a free society;

(*e*) The furtherance of the activities of the United Nations for the Maintenance of Peace." (Adapted from the Plan of Action of the United Nations Decade for Human Rights Education (1995-2004), paragraph 2)

During this Decade, the UN is urging and supporting all member states to make knowledge about human rights available to everyone through both the formal school system and through popular and adult education.

Human Rights Education as a Human Right

Education in human rights is itself a fundamental human right and also a responsibility: the Preamble to the Universal Declaration of Human Rights (UDHR) exhorts "every individual and every organ of society" to "strive by teaching and education to promote respect for these rights and freedoms." The International Covenant on Civil and Political Rights (ICCPR) declares that a government "may not stand in the way of people learning about [their rights]."

Although news reports refer to human rights every day, "human rights literacy" is not widespread in the United States. Students of law and international relations or political science may study human rights in a university setting, but most people receive no education, formally or informally, about human rights. Even human rights activists usually acquire their knowledge and skills by self-teaching and direct experience.

When Americans say, "I've got my rights," they usually think of those civil and political rights defined in the US Bill of Rights, which includes freedom of assembly, freedom of worship, and the right to a fair trial. Few, however, realize that social, economic, and cultural rights such as health care, housing, or a living wage, are also human rights guaranteed in the UDHR.

People who do not know their rights are more vulnerable to having them abused and often lack the language and conceptual framework to effectively advocate for them. Growing consensus around the world recognizes education for and about human rights as essential. It can contribute to the building of free, just and peaceful societies. Human rights education is also increasingly recognized as an effective strategy to prevent human rights abuses.

Rights, Responsibilities and Action

Integral to learning about one's human rights is learning about the responsibilities that accompany all rights. Just as human rights belong to both individuals and society as a whole, the responsibility to respect, defend and promote human rights is both individual and collective. The Preamble of the UDHR, for example, calls not only on governments to promote human rights, but also on "every individual and every organ of society." Human rights education provides the knowledge and awareness needed to meet this responsibility.

The responsibilities of all citizens in a democratic society are inseparable from the responsibility to promote human rights. To flourish, both democracy and human rights require people's active participation. Human rights education includes learning the skills of advocacy - to speak and act every day in the name of human rights.

Human rights education also provides a basis for conflict resolution and the promotion of social order. Rights themselves often clash, such as when one person's commitment to public safety conflicts with another's freedom of expression. As a value system based on respect and the equality and dignity of all people, human rights can create a framework for analyzing and resolving such differences. Human rights education also teaches the skills of negotiation, mediation, and consensus building.

The Goals of Human Rights Education

Human rights education teaches both about human rights and for human rights.

Its goal is to help people understand human rights, value human rights, and take responsibility for respecting, defending, and promoting human rights. An important outcome of human rights education is empowerment, a process through which people and communities increase their control of their own lives and the decisions that affect them. The ultimate goal of human rights education is people working together to bring about human rights, justice, and dignity for all.

Education about human rights provides people with information about human rights. It includes learning - about the inherent dignity of all people and their right to be treated with respect about human rights principles, such as the universality, indivisibility, and inter-dependence of human rights about how human rights promote participation in decision-making and the peaceful resolution of conflicts about the history and continuing development of human rights about international law, like the Universal Declaration of Human Rights or the Convention on the Rights of the Child about regional, national, state, and local law that reinforces international human rights law about using human rights law to protect human rights and to call violators to account for their actions about human rights violations such as torture, genocide, or violence against women and the social, economic, political, ethnic, and gender forces which cause them about the persons and agencies that are responsible for promoting, protecting, and respecting human rights

Education for human rights helps people feel the importance of human rights, internalize human rights values, and integrate them into the way they live. These human rights values and attitudes include:

> "strengthening respect for human rights and fundamental freedoms" (UDHR Article 30.2) nurturing respect for others, self-esteem, and hope understanding the nature of human dignity and respecting the dignity of others empathizing with those whose rights are violated and feeling a sense of solidarity with them recognizing that the enjoyment of human rights by all citizens is a precondition to a just and humane society perceiving the human rights dimension of civil, social, political, economic and cultural issues and conflicts both in the US and other countries valuing non-violence and believing that cooperation is better than conflict.

Education for human rights also gives people a sense of responsibility for respecting and defending human rights and empowers them through skills to take appropriate action. These skills for action include:

recognizing that human rights may be promoted and defended on an individual, collective, and institutional level developing critical understanding of life situations analyzing situations in moral terms realizing that unjust situations can be improved recognizing a personal and social stake in the defense of human rights analyzing factors that cause human rights violations knowing about and being able to use global, regional, national, and local human rights instruments and mechanisms for the protection of human rights strategizing appropriate responses to injustice acting to promote and defend human rights Who Needs Human Rights Education?

Human rights should be part of everyone's education. However, certain groups have a particular need for human rights education: some because they are especially vulnerable to human rights abuses, others because they hold official positions and upholding human rights is their responsibility, still others because of their ability to influence and educate. Among these groups are the following:

Administrators of Justice

- law enforcement personnel, including police and security forces.
- prison officials.
- lawyers, judges and prosecutors.

Other Government and Legislative Officials

- members of the legislature.
- public officials, elected and appointed.
- members of the military.

Other Professionals

- educators.
- social workers.

- health professionals.
- journalists and media representatives.
- Organizations, Associations and Groups.
- women's organizations.
- community activists and civic leaders.
- minority groups.
- members of the business community.
- trade unionists.
- indigenous peoples.
- religious leaders and others with a special interest in social justice issues.
- children and youth.
- students at all levels of education.
- refugees and displaced persons.
- people of all sexual orientations.
- poor people, whether in cities or rural areas.
- people with disabilities.
- migrant workers.

Human rights is not a subject that can be studied at a distance. Students should not just learn about the Universal Declaration, about racial injustice, or about homelessness without also being challenged to think about what it all means for them personally. As human rights educators, we must ask our students and ourselves, "How does this all relate to the way we live our lives?" The answers to this question will tell us much about how effectively we have taught our students.

Conclusion

Any education to be effective needs to be contextualized too. Thus it is not,enough to teach abstract principles of human rights taken from United Nations' documents or our Constitutions. Our historical context as nation as well as local contexts need to be reflected in human rights education. The contextualizing of human rights is essential for nurturing of peace. Creative reflections on local situations from a human rights perspective would help the schools greatly, to become the societies' most important peace makers. Some say that we Indians should have less rights than people living in Western countries. They say, the human rights concepts are Western. Only people who have all the rights could say this to people who have much less rights. We keep masses of humanity without rights and condemn the growing consciousness of rights as a Western one. This would mean that to be Indian one has to put up with one's bondage, one must.

impact of globalization on human rights, 80-81
introduction, 76-77
trade and human rights, 77-80
Dowry Prohibition Act (1961), 73, 103, 165
Durga, S., 32

E

Economic development and human rights, 142-145
economic development and human rights, 143-145
introduction, 142
universal declaration of human rights, 142-143
Empowerment of women, 1-15
constitutional provision, 4-8
laws for working women, 9-15
women empowerment and law, 8-9
Equal Remuneration Act (1976), 165
Equal Remuneration Act, 1976, 9

F

Factories Act, 1984, 10
Family Courts Act (1984), 73
FIDH, 130
Forces influencing human rights in India, 154-158
introduction, 155
reaction to discrimination, rejection, 157
social change and individual role, 156
stigmatization, 156
Foreign Contribution Regulation Act (FCRA), 95
Foreign Marriage Act (1969), 167

G

Gandhi, Indira, 161
Gandhi (Mahatma), 173
Globalisation on human rights, 38-42
Globalization, 32
– and its impact on human rights, 16-24
global activities, 16-23
globalization, development and human rights, 23
introduction, 16
Globalization in India, 130-141
GNP, 76
Government of India, 27, 152

H

Hindu Community, 14
Hindu Marriage Act (1955), 74
Hinduism, 174
HIV/AIDS, 70, 137
HRLN, 70
Human Development Report of 1997, 22
Human Right Cell, 12
Human rights, 38, 76-81, 142-145
Human rights after globalization in India, 130-141
consequences of violations of human rights, 139-140
contradictory basic assumptions, 134-136
globalization and the human rights approach, 140-141
how governments face the contradiction, 136-139
introduction, 130-131
meaning of globalization, 131-134

Human rights and the Indian constitution, 53-65
cultural and educational rights, 61-62
directive principles of state policy, 62-64
fundamental duties, 65
– rights, 58
historical background, 53-56
human rights enshrined in Indian constitution, 57-58
international treaties, 56-57
introduction, 53
right against exploitation, 61
– to constitutional remedies, 62
– – equality, 58-59
– – freedom of religion, 61
– – freedom, 59-61
– – life, 62
Human rights for children in India, 44-52
child rights initiative, 46-47
introduction, 44-45
issues of concern, 45
major aspects to right to education act include, 50-52
– impacts, 45-46
protection of children from sexual offences act, 2012, 50
summary on United Nations convention on the rights of the child, 49-50
teacher convicted for raping a minor student, 47-49
Human rights for women in India, 66-75
constitutional rights to women, 71-72
introduction, 66-67
issues of concern, 69
legal rights to women, 72-75
major impacts, 70-71
what we do, 67-69
women rights in India, 71
Human Rights Forum, 89
Human Rights groups, 13
Human rights in contemporary India, 82-99
challenges, 97
current major areas of research related to human rights, 98
evolution of human rights, 83
fundamental rights vs. human rights, 86-87
human rights violations in India in recent times, 92-97
Magna Carta (1215) was a crucial turning point in the struggle to establish freedom, 83-84
National Human Rights Commission in India, 90-91
remedies, 97-98
status of human rights in India, 87-90
universal declaration of human rights (1948), 84-86
what are human rights, 82-83
Human rights in India, 173-181
administrators of justice, 179
goals of human rights education, 177-179

human rights education
as a human right, 176-177
in India, 174-175
need for human rights education, 173-174
other government and legislative officials, 179
– professionals, 179-180
rights, responsibilities and action, 177
what is human rights education, 175-176
Human rights vs. women rights, 159-162
status of women in India, 161-162
women rights, 159-161

I

ICCPR, 111
ICESCR, 111
IFSW/IASSW, 131
IIMs, 5
IITs, 5
ILO, 35, 137, 148
IMF, 37, 135
Immoral Traffic (Prevention) Act (1956), 72
Impact of globalization on human rights, 32-43
impact of globalisation on human rights, 38-42
international response, 34-38
introduction, 32-34
Indecent Representation of Women (Prohibition) Act (1986), 72
Indian Christian Marriage Act (1872), 74
Indian constitution, 53-65
Indian Penal Code (1860), 73
Information Technology Act, 94
Integrated Child Protection Scheme (ICPS), 27

J

Juvenile Justice Act, 2000, 48

K

Khaps, 93
Kumar, J. Sanath, 151

L

Lakshmi, P. Sunanda Vijaya, 173
Love Commandos, 89

M

Madras Civil Liberties Union, 89
Manikyam, K. Ratna, 44
Marxism, 124
Maternity Benefit Act, 1961, 10, 103
Mauryan, 173
Medical Termination of Pregnancy Act (1971), 73
Mehrotra, Avinash, 45
Mines Act (1952), 74
Misra, Amnuta Rani, 173
Misra, R.N., 82, 159
Misra, Rabi N., 44
Misra, Roopesh Kumar, 16, 130
Moghul, 173
Mother India, 122
Muslim Women in India, 161

N

N.G.O., 13
Naidu, P.L., 53
Naidu, Sarojini, 161
National Building Code of India, 2005, 45

National Commission for Women Act (1990), 75, 167
National Crime Records Bureau (NCRB), 170
National Plan of Action, 25
National Policy for Children, 2013, 29
National Policy for Children, 26
National Women Association, 3
NCRB, 167
New World Order, 76
Newly Industrialized Countries (NIC), 18
NGOs, 67, 97, 103, 146, 147, 175
NIRBHAYA Act, 93

P

Padhal, Puspanjali, 1
Panda, Bandita, 53
Pandit, Vijaya Laxmi, 161
Patnaik, Binayak, 1
Pillai, Priya, 95
PILs, 70
Priyanka, R.J.L.P., 163
Prohibition of Child Marriages Act, 2006, 46, 48
Protection of Women from Domestic Violence Act (2005), 72
Public Interest Cases, 44
Public Interest Litigation (PIL), 15
Purdah and dowry system, 14
Purusha Dharma, 1

R

Raju, Alluri Sitarama, 123
Ram-Gita, 1
Rao, B. Raja, 123
Rao, G. Tirumala Vasu Deva, 154
Rao, K. Venkata, 76
Rao, N. Rajasekhar, 16
Rao, P. Shanmukha, 111
Rashtriya Mahila Kosh, 109
Ratnavalli, B., 32
Reddy, B.R. Prasad, 82
Right to property was originally a fundamental right, but is now a legal right, 62
Role of civil society in protecting the human rights, 146-150
Role of Madduri Annapurnayya in Andhra socialist movement, 123-129
- birth of Andhra congress socialist forum, 124-126
- findings, 128
- Kothapatnam camp, 127
- manthenavaripalem camp, 127-128
- *Nava Sakthi* - Telugu weekly, 126-127

Roy, Raja Ram Mohan, 103

S

SAP, 19
Sasmal, Brajamohan, 100
Satya, V.V., 66
Second World War, 138, 142
Sexual Harassment of Women at Workplace Act (2013), 75
Shah, Amit, 96
Sharma, R.P., 25
Special Marriage Act (1954), 167
Special Taskforce, 44
Sreevaram, T., 159
Stree Dharma, 1
Swamy, Aravind, 146
Swarnalatha, M., 168
Swathi, G., 154

T

Tagore, Rabindra Nath, 15

TINA, 20

TNCs, 34, 40, 79, 137

Tripal Talaqu for Muslim women, 6

U

UNCRC, 49, 50

UNCTAD, 19

UNICEF, 52

Universal Declaration of Human Rights, 11, 99

Universal Declaration, 180

US Bill of Rights (1791), 84

Uttar Pradesh, 93

V

Vedas, 1

Venugopal, S., 142

Vidyasagar, Ishwar Chandra, 103

Vienna Declaration, 1993, 41

Violence against women, 160

Vivekananda, 11

Vivekananda, Swami, 103

W

Wealth of nations, 39

WEDO, 34

Widow Remarriage Act, 1856, 103

Widows and divorcees, 3

Women, 1-15

Women and human rights in India, 168-172

- crimes against women in India, 169-172
- introduction, 168-169

Women empowerment in India, 100-110

- attempts made for empowerment of women by Indian government, 104-110
- introduction, 100-101
- need of women empowerment, 101-102
- possibility of empowerment of women in India, 102-103

Women Justice Initiative (WJI), 67, 68, 69

World Bank, 135

World War II, 35

WTO, 37, 38, 41, 135

Y

YUVA, 148